Write Now!

SOUTH EAST ENGLAND VOL I

Edited by Steve Twelvetree

First published in Great Britain in 2003 by
YOUNG WRITERS
Remus House,
Coltsfoot Drive,
Peterborough, PE2 9JX
Telephone (01733) 890066

All Rights Reserved

Copyright Contributors 2003

SB ISBN 1 84460 217 6

Foreword

This year, Young Writers proudly presents a showcase of the best short stories and creative writing from today's up-and-coming writers.

We set the challenge of writing for one of our four themes - 'Myths & Legends', 'Hold The Front Page', 'A Day In The Life Of . . .' and 'Short Stories/Fiction'. The effort and imagination expressed by each individual writer was more than impressive and made selecting entries an enjoyable, yet demanding, task.

Write Now! South East England Vol I is a collection that we feel you are sure to enjoy - featuring the very best young authors of the future. Their hard work and enthusiasm clearly shines within these pages, highlighting the achievement each piece represents.

We hope you are as pleased with the final selection as we are and that you will continue to enjoy this special collection for many years to come.

CONTENTS

Archbishop Tenison's CE School, Croydon
Sarah Wise	1
Charlie Cox	2
Vasoulla Humphries	4
Steven Little	5
Ben Rosato	6
Laurent Larmond	7
Gemma Gibbs	8
Josephine Backhouse	9
Lloydana Afia Nicholas	10
Lucy Trueick	11

Alwyn Girls' School, London
Pamela Agyemang	12
Tam Thanh Le	12
Shireen Majeed	14
Adefunke Fetuga	15
Kerry Murphy	16
Syrad Douad	17
Harkiran Kaur	18
Ghazal Razvi	20
Angel Namuddu	21
Rose Macharia	22
Margaret Ibiam	24

Bartholomew School, Witney
Katie Stinchcombe	25

Bentley Wood High School, Stanmore
Naveen Ahmad	26
Afrah Jameel	27
Priya Halai	28
Saniya Malik	29

Bishop Challoner RC Upper School, London
- Francesca Kamara — 30
- Tamara Adenuga — 31
- Jamilia Hutchinson — 32
- Benie Nzuzi — 33
- Shaffi Batchelor — 34
- Alice Chen — 35
- Giselle Villanueva — 36

Blenheim High School, Epsom
- Jamie Menditta — 37
- Alice Fenner — 38
- Kayleigh Dray — 39
- Daniel Orton — 40
- Tanaka Samkange — 43

Dedworth Middle School, Windsor
- Charles Oakes — 44
- Sally Poundall — 45
- Joshua Lovell — 46
- George Barlow — 47

Esher CE High School, Esher
- Daniel Hamman — 48
- Daryl Rogers — 50

Glenthorne High School, Sutton
- Kerry Scotney — 53
- Richard Sheehan — 54
- Terry Angell — 55
- David Mew — 56

Harris City Technology College, London
- Laura Bessick — 57
- Aaron Hamilton — 58
- Dion Arthur — 59

Maidstone Grammar School For Girls, Maidstone
- Georgia Colville — 60
- Emily Horgan — 62
- Tabitha Duffield — 66
- Emily Manners — 69

Majorie McClure School, Chislehurst
- Lilly Daisy Cook — 72
- Mark Alan Seagers — 73

Sunnydown School For Boys, Caterham
- Daniel Slack — 74
- Scott Bennett — 76
- Edward Baxter — 77
- Russell Smith — 78
- Ricky Holroyd — 79
- Matthew Bartholomew — 80
- Lee Bainbridge — 81

Sutton High School, Sutton
- Harriette Salvage — 82
- Alexandra Farquharson — 83
- Se-Yi Hong — 84
- Helen Sumping — 85
- Keri Farrow — 86
- Halima Koroma — 87
- Katie Cattell — 88
- Nadia Abdulla — 89
- Amal Khoury — 90
- Sarah Willis — 91
- Jeyhan Mustafa — 92
- Eloise Kohler — 93
- Charlotte Knight — 94
- Rachel Johnston — 95
- Rosanne Erman — 96
- Malini Desai — 97
- Georgina Crate — 98
- Katie Bolton — 99

Franky Gaiger	100
Natasha Dubash	101
Jennifer Crowhurst	102
Melanie Ranaweera	103
Kathy Stevens	104
Jalpa Patel	105
Charmaine Yeoh	106
Nabila Fazal	107
Eleanor Wright	108
Ai Taniuchi	109
Chukwunyere Samuel	110
Sarah Haville	111
Natasha Ward	112
Rebecca Rainback	113
Alice Kendle	114
Claire Caswell	115
Emily Ure	116
Helen McEwan	117
Danielle Tanton	118
Kate Martin	119
Helen Thorpe	120
Charlotte Howson	121
Santina Philips	122
Emy Calder	123
Christina Kang	124
Emma Robertson	125
Lauren Healy	126
Emma Rice	127
Seville Haghbedeh	128
Skeena Hamdani	129
Nancy Godden	130
Catherine Kilkenny	131
Anna Russell	132
Sophie Horgan	133
Laura Hamer	134
Nivedita Chakrabarti	135
Josephine Rawes	136
Louise Privett	137

Fiona Cooper	138
Victoria Hallam	139
Carla Busso	140
Wajeeha Ahmed	141
Priyanka Amin	142
Kathryn Griffiths	143
Seong Won Cha	144
Alexandra San Miguel-Brathwaite	145
Saranya Ravindran	146
Katherine Dart	147
Aarani Sundaram	148
Mei-Lian Hoe	149
Gemma Winters	150
Jessie Cowan	151
Louise Hanger	152
Katie Buckhalter	153
Deborah Farr	154
Esther Nicoll	155
Sana Sheikh	156

Tolworth Girls' School, Sutton
Becky Mayhew	157

Walthamstow School For Girls, Walthamstow
Latoya Walker	158
Mariam Olayiwola	160
Mobheen Sultan	162
Sophia Choudhry	164
Rosa Dudley-Hibbett	166
Sara Akhtar	168
Katie Lewin	170
Emma Louise Pike	172
Francesca Rothkell	174
Merrila Cross	176
Saoirse Kennedy-Barton	178
Saharish Hafeez	180
Charlotte Reynolds	182
Attiya Ahmed	184

Hannah Taylor-Young	186
Aneeka Akhlaq	189
Farah Akhter	190
Louise Bloor	192
Kate Turner	194
Humaa Kazim	196
Maryam Hussain	198
Jennifer Hassan	200

Wesley Green School, Oxford
    Kayleigh Chambers   201

The Creative Writing

MILLIONAIRE ME!

Monday morning and she's still asleep. Eight o'clock came and went, for her, while you kids went to school and started lessons. She's your age but she's not average, like you. She has servants to make her breakfast, do her jobs while she sleeps soundlessly in her designer double bed!

She awakes at about 10 when one of the servants brings her her breakfast in bed! She gets up when she's finished and goes to her pool for a morning swim. When she's done she will have a bath or a shower in the glitz and glam bathroom, whichever she wants, no parents nagging at her heels. She's free to enjoy her day. No work just play, she tells a story in a different way, free from homework and nasty teachers.

She'll have lunch to her plea, anything she wishes has to be, no arguing, fighting or fuss except the fuss people give her!

After lunch she'll go riding or into town. It's what she wants that counts!

When she's back she'll have a snack of her choice and when her friends come over they go to her lounge with a buffet and any great game, you name it, she's got it.

When they're hungry, all of them can pick and take what they want, no being told what to eat or what not to eat! No adults to say: 'Eat your greens,' or, 'no more pudding for you.'

After that they will have an evening swim, then they will go home and she'll go to her room to watch a film or just the TV. She'll go to bed at her own wish, no one will tell her!

That's a day in the life of millionaire me!

Sarah Wise (13)
Archbishop Tenison's CE School, Croydon

CHICKEN BOY

'You want me to what!'
'That's right chicken boy, to prove you're not a chicken, hunt the dragon in that cave.'
'But it's impossible, many have gone to fight it and died, and they were grown men!'
'So you are not a chicken then?'
'No I am not, I have a name remember, Andy.'
'Oh yeah, Andy-chicken boy.'
'*No!* My name is Andy Jones and if it makes you happy then I will do this dare.'
'Oh it'll make me happy alright, happy to see you die.'

Now what you have to understand is that, well Andy is a chicken, but he just didn't like being called a chicken. So anyone who liked him didn't call him a chicken. So naturally there is always one who doesn't like him, plus his demented followers who say things like, 'Oh ha ha, great one boss.' This person's name was Bad Boy Brad. Or you can just call him Brad.

So after accepting his mission Andy went into the dragon's cave. All he could smell was fear and death. As he progressed through the cave it became a long winding tunnel. All of a sudden he tripped on something, so he got out a torch from his bag and looked at what it was he'd tripped on. When he did he was sick, it was the remains of one of the men who'd come to face the dragon, but it was no longer a man, it was just a rotting piece of flesh.

At this moment he realised that he could be next. The next person to be devoured then have maggots and flies all over his rotting corpse. When he had stopped puking he proceeded on.

After about ten minutes he came to a clearing, where he found the dragon asleep. Then it struck him, he had no weapon, how was he going to beat the beast?

After all this time thinking he didn't notice the dragon had awoken. It gave an almighty roar before walking up to Andy. Then he remembered there was a sword by the bit of rotting flesh. He turned to run and ran into the wall. He was cornered. As he stared the dragon in the eyes he realised this dragon was no threat. It was just protecting itself. The dragon roared again, protection or not Andy knew it was his time . . .

Charlie Cox (12)
Archbishop Tenison's CE School, Croydon, Croydon

A Day In The Life Of Fame

A girl called Sophia was at a concert when she imagined she was a superstar. All of a sudden the pop star pulled her up on stage and asked her if she would join in with them and sing along to the words. 15 minutes later it had all finished.

Then the next week she was at home in her garden, sunbathing because it was a very hot day, so she fell asleep. She thought to herself, *I wish I could be a superstar.*

All of a sudden she woke up and she was in another world. She said, 'What am I doing here? I don't belong here!'
A voice spoke, 'You are a superstar in the Fame kingdom.'
Sophia spoke, 'But why?'
The voice said, 'Because you wished for it and it has come true.'

Sophia was amazed at what happened. She thought to herself, *What shall I do first?* First she went and got pampered at the beauty salon. After she came out she went to the posh shops and got herself some clothes. She spent £300! After, she went to the shoe shop and saw a lovely pair of shoes and she bought them. She thought to herself, *this is the life.* After she went back to the palace and she said to the voice, 'Thank you very, very much, I have had the time of my life.'

She closed her eyes and said, 'I wish I could be back home, 1, 2, 3, 4.'

20 minutes later she was back home in the garden. She looked on the floor and all the bags were there. She said that it was very *bizarre.*

Vasoulla Humphries (13)
Archbishop Tenison's CE School, Croydon

GOODBYE

This morning I just said goodbye to my dad who was going to fight in the Gulf war. I am really scared because I don't know whether he will ever come back, alive. When I was saying goodbye I had to walk away because I was so sad about seeing my dad go, I just couldn't take it. Whenever I watch the news I have to go to my room because I sometimes see my dad in the background, but if I don't see him, all of the soldiers remind me of him. I hear on the news that people have been killed and every time I just wish it is not my dad, because if he did ever die I don't know what I would do without him.

A week after I said goodbye to my dad we got a telephone call from him. I was so happy to hear he was okay. He told me that he couldn't be long so we had to make it quick. I could not stop saying how much I missed him. I spent about a minute talking to him and then my mum spoke to him. When he had to go I kept on thinking whether he was ever going to call back. I was so pleased that he was fine.

That night me and my mum went to a restaurant to celebrate that he was okay, but when we got back we got a message that said he'd had an accident. My mum then called them back up and said that she wanted to know what had happened. All I heard from my bedroom was my mum crying her eyes out. I went down and said, 'What's wrong Mum?' and she told me that while Dad was about to raid one of the Iraq camps, someone had snuck up behind him and stabbed him to death. One of the men he went with went back to the main camp and said that five of them had been killed and the guy who reported it just made it out alive.

Steven Little (12)
Archbishop Tenison's CE School, Croydon

A Day In The Life Of A Soldier

My name is Bill Jones, I've been out in Iraq for a couple of months now, not fighting, just preparing to fight. But now the day has come for the RAF to bomb Baghdad. I fly a Tornado and I treat it like a pet. Last night I polished her up till she looked brand new. I ain't looking forward to this but it's my duty and I just try to think to myself that I'm fighting for my country and for the Iraqi civilians. My father fought in the Gulf war and told me all about his adventures and of course Saddam Hussein! Saddam is Iraq's evil leader. There are about four Tornadoes going out today and our job is to locate and destroy Saddam's palaces. Wish me luck!

I am just four miles away from Baghdad. I can just see the edge of the city, time to fire a warning missile. As I fire I feel the power and speed of it rock my plane, a few seconds later I hear a rumble as it sprays rocks and rubble away from the destroyed church. I fly over it and go speeding past other buildings. Then I see it, my heart leaps two beats as I catch a glimpse of one of Saddam's palaces. I launch a missile at its side and with a boom it collapses to its foundations.

'Nice shooting. Pull out, the other planes have taken the rest out,' that was the voice of the military leader, he was in charge of our mission. My job here is done!

Ben Rosato (13)
Archbishop Tenison's CE School, Croydon

AMERICA AND BRITAIN DEFEAT IRAQ

Only survivor out of the people who went to Baghdad: Laurent Larmond, aged 13.

I went into Baghdad with three other soldiers. It was all up to the three of us to do our mission. As soon as we walked 30 metres into Baghdad my friend Billy got snipered, so John and I ran for cover. Luckily there was an old truck still there from the Gulf war. So we hid behind that. We stayed there until he stopped shooting then we got up and straight away he shot again, but luckily it missed. Then I took out my gun and straight away I saw him. The good news was that he was reloading, the bad news was that he had nearly finished. So me and my friend John both shot him down. He had two bullet shots in his forehead and to make it worse he dropped off the tower that was about 100 metres in the sky. To make it even worse, he landed head first.

Then me and my friend made a run for it to a closer port of cover. Then another run and then another run until we were close enough to see where people were. There were two men standing next to a tank, so I took out my rocket launcher and blew them and the tank to pieces. There was no chance of any of them surviving.

Suddenly two men came behind us and told us to put our hands in the air and drop our guns. So we did but when both guns had dropped, two bullets were fired and the two Iraqi men dropped to the floor. I looked up and I saw a fighter jet in the sky.

Laurent Larmond (13)
Archbishop Tenison's CE School, Croydon

PEACE PARTY

'Get down, quickly,' said Soldier Myley.
'What are you on about Myley, the war is over!'
'Don't be ridiculous it has barely started. How can it be finished?'
'It just is, come back to base and see for yourself!'
Soldier Myley just did not believe Soldier Rusby that the war was over. When they got back to base everyone was silent yet screaming! All their faces as bright as a sunflower!
'The war is over!' they all said in unison.
Myley could not believe his ears for the second time! 'Really?' said Myley.
'Really!' they said in unison again.
Everyone hugged each other and jumped about like children! 'Let's go home,' they said and all agreed. On the way home everyone was watching the telly and ringing their loved ones.

When they arrived in England, on the fifth day of being home, everyone went up to London to have a peace party! Everyone bought a peace balloon. As they counted down from 100-1, It felt great for the soldiers, only unusual. It was only an unusual sensation though, as they were counting down to peace instead of war! 150,768 balloons were let go. That was only the amount in this country, let alone all the other countries!

Soldier Myley held his baby. Her soft skin, her friendly smile and sweet smell. He held his wife close as well, not forgetting her love. In all of this he would never forget who pulled him through this terrifying adventure.

Gemma Gibbs (12)
Archbishop Tenison's CE School, Croydon

THE NIGHT CASTLE

It looked like an ordinary castle from the outside, it had brown walls, a large door and cobwebs in the corner. There wasn't anything mysterious or scary.

Nikitta Blake was one of the few people who lived in the village who wasn't terrified of the castle. She didn't believe that it was haunted and she would have loved to go inside. Nikitta was fiery and determined. She had long, red, curly hair cascading almost to her waist and large green eyes. She loved a challenge.

She knew her gran would never let her go to the castle, so Nikitta knew she would have to sneak out. Choosing a day was hard, on Fridays they always went to see Grandad in hospital and on Tuesday Gran's friend came round. Eventually she chose Thursday afternoon when Gran would be resting, Nikitta knew she wouldn't be missed.

On Thursday afternoon Nikitta was standing at the door of the castle looking for a handle, there didn't seem to be one, so she pushed the door expecting it to be locked. It wasn't and it creaked open slowly. Nikitta took a deep breath and went in. It was pitch-black, so Nikitta switched on her torch. It was very dusty inside and the wooden floorboards creaked loudly when she stepped on them.

Suddenly she heard a noise above her and she shone her torch up and then she screamed as all the evil things came out . . .

Josephine Backhouse (13)
Archbishop Tenison's CE School, Croydon

YOUNG SOLDIER

Bang! Bang! The young soldier ran anxiously across the desolate battlefields wondering if he could make it. All around him was nothing but death and destruction. Dry rotting carcasses littered the dirty, rat-infested floor. Excited insects and vermin swarmed over the dead bodies creating a pungent, putrid smell. The smell seemed almost unbearable but the soldier seemed not to notice. His appearance, although highly masculine and fierce, was simply a mask to hide his ever-fluctuating fear.

As he hid between the bushes near the border of Kuwait, he thought about his family. His wife had only recently given birth to their two-week-old baby, Charlotte. How he yearned to see her, to feel her soft baby skin and to watch her dazzling smile: he loved her innocence.

He thought of his wife Sheila. He wanted so badly to hold her in his arms again or to see her face. As he thought about her, his heart weakened with joy at the thought of her love.

The young soldier thought about George Bush. How could he do this to him? Did the officials not understand that people have lives to live? In his opinion the war was selfish and without motive. He hated George Bush for bringing this level of Hell and damnation upon him.

Lloydana Afia Nicholas (12)
Archbishop Tenison's CE School, Croydon

A DAY IN THE LIFE OF A WRITER

I surreptitiously stifle a cough as the sweaty armpit of the waiter is shoved up against my nose when he forcibly slams down another watery tea onto the already chipped Formica table. The sound does nothing to ease my pulsing headache.

'Thanks,' I give him a smile almost as weak as the liquid in front of me. Almost, but not quite. I stir in two sugars and curse as yet another drip of tea splatters onto my already blemished notebook, rendering the title almost illegible.

Concentrate. The word flashes in bold type inside my head. I purposefully flip open the notebook and scrabble through the rubble in my bag to find a Biro. I sit, waiting for inspiration . . . but nothing comes. My gaze lingers on the far wall of the café, the grimy floral flock of the walls and the gilt frame paintings, strategically placed to hide the damp, do nothing to improve my mood. The whirr of the central heating system resounds in my head, although blowing billows of grey dust around the room is more its forte rather than actually heating. The inspiration I wait for is in regard to the last chapter of my book you see - I can't think of an ending - *so* frustrating.

The insistent sound of metal upon metal tells me the chairs are being stacked up, it's time to go home. Another unproductive day. Will this book about a magical world and its young wizard star Harry *ever* be finished? I know it's a long shot but I'd love to have it published someday.

Well, we can all dream, can't we . . .
J K Rowling.

Lucy Trueick (16)
Archbishop Tenison's CE School, Croydon

THE SECRET GARDEN

This story book is about a girl called Mary Lennox, who was sent to Miss Elthwaite's manor to live with her uncle. Everybody said she was 'the most disagreeable-looking child ever seen'. Mary's little face was yellow because she had been born in India. It was written by Frances Hodgson Burnett.

This book is a mystery book, because this young girl call Mary had found a hidden secret door that lead her to the mysterious garden, but the garden was dirty.

The plot involves Mary waking up one morning and she became angrier till she saw that the servant who stood by her was not her good servant Ayah. Mary shouted, 'Send my Ayah.'

Mary is my favourite character in the book because she found the mysterious hidden garden. Mary made the story more funny and sad and she made it the best story to read. Mary was good because she was a good person.

The best part is when she found the key to the mysterious hidden secret door and when she met Dickon who was in magic communication with animals. Colin, her invalid cousin is cured by the magical powers that's in him.

I will recommend this book by saying, everybody has to buy one and it will be more exciting to read, but it is a bit terrifying. I would recommend it to everyone because this book is really good, that is why I chose to write about it.

Pamela Agyemang (11)
Aylwin Girls' School, London

WRITING A REVIEW

The name of the play I've watched is 'Race To Change Face'. In the play, there are two men and two women. Their names are Jason, Rezaj, Pearl and Malikey. I saw this play in school with all the other year sevens.

This play is an action play because it is about fighting for their rights. It's got a bit of romance in it too. I think this play is for teenagers.

Pearl is Jason's big sister. Their dad died. They think some joyriders killed him but they don't know for sure. Pearl has kept lots of secrets from Jason. Jason joins a gang in Angle Town. Jason meets a really nice girl, who is white. She is a refugee.

My favourite character is Rezaj. Her real name is Joy. Rezaj is a fantastic actor and she is funny. Rezaj has long blonde hair, blue eyes and a round face. She is from England and is 21 years old. Rezaj is a bit short though.

The best bit was when they were fighting. The funniest part was when Jason and Rezaj bumped into each other. Then they started making friends, but the saddest bit was when they were talking about how their dad died.

I would recommend this play to people over eight because it's not about children's or grown-up stuff. It's all about racism. This play is teaching us about racism and it teaches us that we shouldn't judge people because of their colour.

Tam Thanh Le (12)
Aylwin Girls' School, London

TITANIC

The film is called 'Titanic', the main actor is Leonardo Di Caprio who plays Jack. The main actress is Kate Winslet who plays Rose. I saw it on video at home. I was with my three cousins. The cover shows 'Titanic' in the background and Rose and Jack standing on Titanic. It is based on real life.

I think it's romantic because when the lifeboats are ready to leave for the women, Rose (Kate Winslet) doesn't go on because she wants to stay with Jack (Leonardo Di Caprio).

Historians are looking for the 'heart of the ocean'. A woman knows about the 'heart' and she wants to see her picture which a boy drew for her wearing the 'heart of the ocean'. The woman tells the historians about the 'heart of the ocean' and how it all happened.

My favourite character is Jack because he's poor. His parents have died and he gambles. He wins two tickets to America and on the boat he meets Rose and after a while they fall in love. Then comes disaster.

The saddest scene is when Jack dies. He dies because there were not enough lifeboats for them. Jack saves Rose from drowning and he dies himself in freezing water.

I think this film is excellent as it has feeling and emotions. This film is recommended for adults but it's written on the cover as a 12 certificate. The reason I think it's for adults is because it's a romance.

Shireen Majeed (11)
Aylwin Girls' School, London

WRITING A REVIEW FOR 'SLEEPOVER'

The book is about a girl called Daisy who has lots of friends. Their names are Amy, Chloe, Bella, Kate and Emily. I read this book when I was at home. I read the book for homework. The book is covered in blue, red and white, the same as the back. The person that wrote this book is called Jacqueline Wilson.

This book is a teenager's book because almost all teenagers sleep over in their friends' houses. There they have presents and treats.

Something bad happens in the story. Daisy tries to be Emily's best friend but Chloe the bossy one won't let them be best friends.

The funniest part was when Daisy's dad tried to bang a hammer on Chloe's head. The saddest part was when Chloe said Daisy couldn't come to her sleepover party. The best part was when Emily shouted at Chloe at Daisy's sleepover party.

My favourite character is Emily. She dresses smart, she has short hair, she is tall, she's always happy, she is also friendly and pretty. She has a fringe, she's clever and has a slim head. Emily has skinny legs and fat toes and big toenails.

I would recommend this for teenagers and young girls because it's all about sleepovers and parties about sleepovers. Aged nine to thirteen will be good for the book because over thirteens will think it is boring for them and they would call it a baby story.

Adefunke Fetuga (12)
Aylwin Girls' School, London

WRITING A REVIEW

The best film I have seen is 'Bend It Like Beckham'. It's about a girl who loved to play football. I saw the film at the cinema. I was with my class friends.

I think that 'Bend it Like Beckham' is a romance because people fall in love and it's a teenage thing because it is funny. It makes me feel this way because I always laugh through it and the people in the film love each other.

The girl wants to be a footballer and her parents don't want her to because of her religion, so then she meets someone that she falls in love with and wants to get married. But her mum and dad get so angry and stop them so they leave it for the moment and later they get married.

The girl is always doing something like playing football, going out without telling her mum and she always gets what she wants.

The funniest bit is when she goes to take a shot and her family are in the goal moving around saying, 'Don't do it! Do it for me!' and she takes it. The saddest bit is when her and her best friend break up when her friend finds out that she has been kissing her boyfriend, well the one she really likes and the girl knows that. I would recommend it to little kids who enjoy romance and action.

Kerry Murphy (12)
Aylwin Girls' School, London

A Day In The Life Of A War Victim (Second World War)

Early morn, I have nowhere to go. No home, no family, no friends. It has all been taken away from me.

I can only sit in a pitch-black toilet of a house which long ago was a loving home. I can hear chattering. Plans to wipe out people like me, people with no reasons to live anymore, no significance, people with nothing!

I was nearly seized by a Nazi soldier . . . my heart racing to the point I could not breathe gave him the impression I was already dead. I almost wish I was. It is my birthday already.

The bombs that shower the smoky grey sky are my fireworks. But they have no colour, no warmth, no happiness. It is dinner time. I can tell because Nazi soldiers nearby are feasting on rice, chicken, vegetables and coffee. My nose has become killer-sensitive. My mouth is a puddle of water dripping down to my chin. The growling of my stomach is one of a killer woodland bear. I am dangerously hungry!

I get the feelings these are my final days. I will soon be reunited with my family in a place far, far away.

I can only sit and pray one day differences will become a silent discussion, not a bloody, unmerciful war.

Syrad Douad (12)
Aylwin Girls' School, London

LUNCH MANIA

Mayhem at lunch, in Waverley Girls'.

At Waverley Girls' school in Bermondsey we have heard that the school has employed two criminals who have been in really bad trouble in the last 10 years.

It has been a panic for Waverley's head teacher Mrs Johnard, a tall, skinny woman. Staff who have worked at Waverley and who are there now are shocked and have been so frightened that the school has had to be closed now and will stay closed for the remaining two weeks.

The two women Ms Vera and Ms Tammy had been to jail twice and have got a criminal record, but Waverley has been fooled as well as being dumb. Ms Vera, aged 46 now, went to jail at the age of 12 for shoplifting for four years! While Ms Tammy, aged 44, was put in jail at the age of two years for stealing one sweet that she couldn't afford. The two became friends as they were put in the same jail and the same cell!

The two of them, not having references, had been put in jail for another few years for being bad citizens and also for breaking into every store in Mayfair, well almost every store for they got caught just before doing the second to last!

'Obviously they did not get married nor have children. For that record they are just a couple of idiots who should be jailed for life after all they have done!' quoted one woman.

The people of the *The Khalsa Newspaper* are shocked at Waverley and amazed at the head teacher! We have never heard of a school who have employed anyone without a reference!

Anyway this is how the whole story began. Two girls had caught the two dinner ladies putting poison, which forensics have told police is green venom from a highly poisonous snake, in the dinners! These two ladies have been found guilty by the fingerprints for trying to poison a school of high achievers! The school has now reopened with a new head teacher named Ms Williams, but a lot of people have to laugh at the person who was responsible for putting their school in danger by employing two criminals! The evidence in their writing plan was to take the school in their control by poisoning everyone and taking their money and supplies that they needed. They have also killed at least two children who had the poison at breaktime by different fumes.

Harkiran Kaur (12)
Aylwin Girls' School, London

IMAX

A total massacre. The gas had not yet dispersed. The dead bodies of bloodied soldiers filled the field. The debris of blasted tanks, armoured troop carriers and other war materials littered the battlefield as if it was a huge junkyard.

Funny; we knew the enemy too well. Yet we never came across the idea of a surprise attack. If we had, we would have been on alert. Yet, looking around, the death toll would be too high, even for a war like this. The bodies of the soldiers were scattered around as if on a board game. If this were a film it would have got five stars, not to mention an Oscar. But it was now time for the cast to get up and take a break. Yet not one leg twitched; not one head looked up.

Ghazal Razvi (13)
Aylwin Girls' School, London

THE DEATH OF STARDUST MONROE

I'm very cynical about death. I'm not religious so I think that when you die, *that's it!* You've gone, your body will rot, you will not exist any more, I don't believe in the afterlife either.

Stardust Monroe had the same views, she didn't mind what happened *after* she died, she was reaching her prime and wanted to go out in style. She didn't have a boring life and she sure didn't want a boring death. Unlike most, she planned her death. The death itself wasn't going to be the spectacular part, but the way she would be found: in a bed of roses in a luxurious nighty, *dead*. The most important part of her death would be people knowing, what's a performer without an audience? Stardust called the news crew with a promise of a juicy story; the reporters said they would meet her on a Sunday, so that that was the fixed day of her death.

Everything went to plan, Sunday came and so did the news crew, but the problem was there was no one to let them in.

A month passed and Stardust's neighbour, a more plainly named Stuart called the news crew about a strange smell coming from next door, the reporters said they would come on Sunday. Sunday came and so did the news crew, and police, for the smell, and there before their eyes they saw a decayed Stardust *dead* in a bed of *dead* roses.

Stardust died knowing she'd be famous.

Angel Namuddu (13)
Aylwin Girls' School, London

THE CULT MURDERS

Inspector Adams grimly approached the crime scene looking pitifully at the dead body. The young man was approximately twenty-one years old, dressed in a black robe and on his left arm was the mark of a ram cruelly carved into his naked flesh. He knew now why he was called to the scene.

For the past five years he'd been investigating some cult murders, ever since he'd found his niece killed in a similar manner. So far he'd found nothing, only that the victims were randomly picked and had nothing in common. Adams slowly made his way to his car. Sitting back as his eyes drooped lower and lower, Adam fell into a deep sleep as he envisioned his niece's last moments in life . . .

Janet looked around at the dark room. The air was stale, giving her the distinct feeling of death. She'd been here for a few hours, waiting to find out what would happen. She sat down trying to calm herself, when suddenly she wished she was with her Uncle Adam, they were close.

She had everything that she'd taken from college; so she decided to use the tape recorder in her pocket. She wanted someone to know what had happened if she didn't survive.

The door opened, showing a sturdy figure approaching. As she turned on the tape recorder, she knew that she wouldn't live through this. They took her to a bath filled with what smelt like herbs and salts. Women came in and washed her with a look of sadness on their faces, as if they were pained by what she'd be going through. Finally they put a black robe on her. Later, having been slightly sedated, she saw the knife glint in the darkness as they came slowly towards her. She felt the knife pierce through her skin as they carved something on her arm ignoring her shattering screams. Having endured enough, she slipped into unconsciousness.

As the chants grew stronger, she prayed. The sharp knife came down, cutting cleanly through her heart when she muttered, 'Father, forgive my sins.' The tears she had wept froze on her pale cheeks, as she tumbled into darkness.

Rose Macharia (14)
Aylwin Girls' School, London

INTO CARE

I'm fourteen years old and I have been living in care for as long as I can remember. I have no family who live in the UK. My mother died when she gave birth to me as for my father, he ran away with a chambermaid! I used to live with my Aunt Celia but she found her dream man and sent me into care.

My school is a typically mixed school, girls who wear skirts short enough to be belts and boys who smoke weed. My social worker says my behaviour is improving, so I could soon find a foster family.

I've only lived with one foster family but they sent me back because I was too dark to blend in with their skin colour; (they were racists).

I only have a few friends in my school; Jayda is my best friend, she told me her mum is thinking of fostering me. Jayda said her mum is a social worker and works in foster homes around London.

I've been suspended for abusing another pupil, Jayda asked her mum to speak to me about my behaviour. She said she might think of fostering me if my behaviour improved. I've started to turn into a geek and I'm frightening my friends off with my good behaviour but at least I'm close to having a foster family.

Jayda has some good news for me - *I have a foster family!*

I'm literally over the moon, but I'm not sure whether it will last.

Margaret Ibiam (12)
Aylwin Girls' School, London

TRIXIE LIXIE THE MAGIC PIXIE AND THE GNOME!

Trixie Lixie lives at the end of a beautiful garden in the middle of a sunflower, with her sister Mary May. A lovely old lady called Mrs Price owns the garden.

One day Mrs Price went shopping with her daughter to buy some plants. Whilst they were gone Trixie Lixie and Mary May fluttered around the garden playing with little berries, using them as balls. Whilst they were having fun, Mrs Price returned with an odd statue . . .

Trixie poked her head out from between two petals and stared at this statue. After a few minutes, she flew out and started to go over, Mary May followed. Then they paused, Trixie edged closer wanting a better look. Then Mary May remembered a book she'd read all about a pixie being lost because a gnome had stolen her . . . *this was a gnome!*

Suddenly the gnome came to life and grabbed Trixie and threw her into his bag just as Mrs Price came outside. Mary May wasn't sure what to do! She flew back to their sunflower to get her wand and do what she thought was best.

Mary May rushed back, hoping she wasn't too late. She recited a spell she hoped would work:
> 'A gnome has caught Trixie tight,
> Please rescue her from her plight.
> Remove his bag, soft and swift,
> So Trixie can be free.
> 1 . . . 2 . . . 3 . . . *Lift!*'

The bag dropped and out tumbled Trixie.
'I'm free!' cried Trixie.
'Phew!' sighed Mary, 'let's go home!'

Katie Stinchcombe (13)
Bartholomew School, Witney

A Day In The Life Of A Soldier
In The Second World War

The sky so dark, so miserable and so cold, closes in on me and my fellow soldiers. I am sitting in the freezing, musty, smelly campsite with no possessions but a helmet, gas mask and rifle. The rest of the soldiers are in a deep slumber but I lie waiting and wondering about the situation in which I am in and why I am in it! All I wonder about is not how we are going to conquer these evil, immortal, death lovers but about my family back home.

I have no way of contacting them. There is a constant pain which remains in me, this stabbing pain of immense misery, takes over me. The pain will not go until I find myself close to my family and sometimes I think I will have the pain inside me until I am dead and buried.

Every single day in which I am involved, is a repetition of the same activities. I never know what could happen in the next second, we are all waiting until most of our soldiers die from being loyal and staying true till the very end for Britain.

The world in which I live is not a safe world, I imagine it as a second Hell. I cannot breathe normally, I am henceforth a prisoner.

As soon as the break of dawn arrives, suddenly fear helps my hands and knees knock against each other. I desperately try and alert myself to focus on what could be the last time I see daylight.

Neveen Ahmad (15)
Bentley Wood High School, Stanmore

A Day In The Life Of Medusa

I wake up slowly, trying to keep my eyes shut for longer, holding on to my dream, where I am normal, plain, boring and most importantly with boring people. Unfortunately I can't sleep through the day as I am awoken by my hissing, slippery hair. The first thing I usually do is fill the sink with water to wash with, sometimes I scare myself. However this immediately brings me back to reality and I remember who I am. I am the world-famous Medusa and I will turn anyone who dares to look into my eyes, into stone, nothing more than a lifeless statue.

Slowly eating breakfast I plan what to do with myself. Usually I stay at home on my large estate which I claimed several centuries ago and wander through the grounds, my 'hair' loves the fresh air.

I enjoy reading fiction stories in the evenings where people have friends that are always there for them and where men look into women's eyes and whisper sweet nothings. But sometimes I can't stand reading those fairy stories, where people live happily ever after, because it will never happen, at least not to me. Imagine if someone ever actually liked me and wanted to tell me something as they looked into my eyes, they would simply be turned into a pile of rubble and kept on the side with the rest of them. It's actually quite funny when you think about it!

When late evening comes I get bored and through my telescope I watch people carrying on with their mundane lives, having always to be nice and polite to other people, although they're not always nice back. Being continuously told what to do by nuisance friends and family. I am much happier than they are; I'm famous, have a wonderful home, have anything I please and no one ever dares mess with me!

I usually go to bed early, I look forward to the time when I'm not bothered by these creatures resting on my head. I fall asleep hoping for some bizarre reason that I am one of those boring people I see through my telescope - or at least I dream I am.

Afrah Jameel (16)
Bentley Wood High School, Stanmore

THE YOUNG WARRIOR

Noise swept across the deep Amazonian jungle as the leader of the Nairo tribe gave his final speech. His son Mairo stared at the immense presence of his father as he talked about the close upcoming war. Mairo hated war, the thought made him feel insecure and flooded him with great weakness. Yet his father's words were strong and comforted Mairo and the other villagers.

The village warriors had been preparing for war and, although just twelve, Mairo had been obliged to learn his father's ways and would fight alongside the older warriors. It was today Mairo felt a slight unease inside him, the steady pace of the forest's routine had been disrupted and he could sense what was to come.

An immense amount of rain fell as villagers ate their morning meal. At that moment a roar spread across the forest floor and a nearby tribe began their invasion in a desperate battle for land. Mairo stood tall behind his father as the battle began. Mairo had never seen so much pain and so much death but was encouraged to defend his land. The rains continued and so did the battle until all was still. The Nairo warriors had been victorious.

Yet all was not well, as in the battle the life of the Nairo tribe's great leader had been lost. A poisonous arrow had struck his heart in the great struggle for victory. His body lay peacefully on the freed land. Mairo's tears fell upon his father's body and the strains of his people fell upon Mairo's shoulders as he took his place as the new leader.

Priya Halai (16)
Bentley Wood High School, Stanmore

AN INNOCENT LIFE

The summer months arrived and Daniel, a three-year-old toddler, loved the outdoors. Every day with his mother, he would go to pick his sisters up from school.

It was a hot summer's day, Daniel and his mother were out as usual to pick up his sisters. Daniel loved ice cream, his mum bought him one and he sat there covering his face with ice cream which made him all sticky. His mum got angry, which made him upset and restless.

The hot blazing sun shone on him and the heat made him uncomfortable. He cried and moved about in his pram wanting to get out, so he started playing with his belt.

Being a clever little boy, he managed to undo himself from his pram and he ran. Not looking where he was going, Daniel ran on to the busy main road. A car was coming along, speeding down, the driver, not having enough time to stop, hit Daniel and he went down with a thump.

His horrified mother stood there screaming as she watched her child on the floor. Daniel was taken into the Emergency Room, but later died in hospital with severe injuries.

Saniya Malik (16)
Bentley Wood High School, Stanmore

THESIUS AND THE CAVE OF RICHES

Thesius was a very poor man who had to feed a family of six. He made his money by doing chores, this helped Thesius and his family but it was barely enough, because people gave him half the money he asked for.

One day Thesius was walking, thinking about his problems, when he stumbled over a map. Being witless he followed the map and ended up at a cave. He pushed the cave door but it wouldn't budge. Thesius asked passers-by if they knew about the map, but they knew nothing.

Men dressed in black strolled by and Thesius asked them and one angrily replied,
'I, Persian, will have your head if you don't give me that map!'
Trembling, Thesius ran away.

That night, Thesius went back, Persian was there with three other men so Thesius hid.
Persian stood in front of the cave and slowly said,
'Cave! Like an arc,
Keeping everything inside safe and sacred.
Night sky,
Give us light that will delight!'

The cave opened and they all went inside.

To Thesius's amazement, the light was the riches, beaming radiantly.

Later Persian and his men came out and Persian said the complete opposite and the cave closed.

Minutes after they left, Thesius spoke Persian's words and the cave opened again. When Thesius came out he was hung, drawn and quartered by Persian's men.

They do say that if you go to that cave in India you can still hear Thesius wailing in pain and agony.

Francesca Kamara (12)
Bishop Challoner RC Upper School, London

A Day In The Life Of The Beckhams

David and Victoria were woken up by a high-pitched scream made by baby Romeo. Brooklyn woke up crying because he'd had a nightmare. As soon as David was able to calm down Brooklyn and Victoria was able to make Romeo be quiet, the family went downstairs to have some breakfast. David had bacon, egg and sausages. Victoria had a healthy shake and Alpen. Brooklyn had Coco Pops and Romeo just had milk.

David's breakfast was disturbed by an important phone call saying there was a big football match that day against Chelsea in London at 1pm. David told Victoria that they were all going to London for the big match.

Victoria got ready as fast as she could, then she got the boys ready. Victoria and David got into an argument because David was taking his time getting ready and Victoria wanted to get down to London early so that she could go to the West End to do some shopping.

By the time they got to London it was 11.45pm. The Beckhams signed themselves into their hotel and then went straight down to the West End.

David bought himself a new watch from New Bond Street and Victoria bought a new bag from Louis Vuitton. They bought Brooklyn a new car game for his Game Boy Advance. Romeo got a big teddy bear which could walk and talk and which was bigger than he was.

At the match, Manchester United won 3-0. David scored 2 and Ruud van Nistelrooy scored 1. The Beckhams went home happy.

Tamara Adenuga (11)
Bishop Challoner RC Upper School, London

THE FIRST FALL OUT

Hi! I'm going to tell you a little story about three best friends and an unexpected fall out.

It all started on Saturday night when three best friends, Sue, Natasha and Jamilia decided to have a sleepover and as usual it was round at Sue's house because she had the biggest bedroom.

They had just finished watching a scary film when Sue smartly suggested that they should play a friendship game and everyone agreed, so she began to set it up. When Sue had set the game up, they began to play.

Further into the game a question came up, it was to say what your friend's best speciality was. It was Natasha who had to go first, she chose singing for Jamilia and acting for Sue.

Sue then chose dancing for Jamilia and being dumb for Natasha.

Lastly Jamilia's turn came and she chose acting for Sue and being dumb for Natasha. Natasha steamed up with anger and blamed the issue all on Jamilia.

You'll be happy to know that they did make up the following morning, which shows that they are true friends and that it was all a silly misunderstanding. So don't make the same mistake as they did or it may mean your friendship is at risk!

Jamilia Hutchinson (11)
Bishop Challoner RC Upper School, London

A Day In The Life Of An Iraqi Girl

My name is Love, I come from Iraq and I am twelve years old. You may be wondering how I can be in Iraq and have an English name! Well my dad went to study medicine in the UK but unfortunately he died during the Gulf War when Saddam used poisonous gasses in Kuwait. My dad was to visit the family of the boy I was betrothed to.

I am an only child and I have a mum called Nasira, who is thirty years old. Every day our hatred for Saddam gets bigger. So I was glad to hear that the Americans and the coalition forces were fighting to stop Saddam's regime and for him to leave his position as president. I was also very scared and worried, as any other person would be, about what would happen if my family was besieged or if we ran out of food and water?

I don't go to school as I help my mum around the house. Once when I was going out to collect some water for my mum, I saw one of the ground troops from the coalition forces, he was giving out some food and drink to the children. It was expected to last us for a whole month!

When I got home I showed my mum the gift I had got from one of the ground troops, she was very grateful. We prayed to thank God that He and the military were fighting for our liberation and freedom.

I want to be a doctor in England when I grow up, I just hope my life won't be cut short because of this war. When Saddam goes, I will feel safe again.

Benie Nzuzi (12)
Bishop Challoner RC Upper School, London

WHY WHALES SING

Aeons ago, before the wind blew and the stars lit up our sky, the Earth was just water. In that water lived the mermaids. They lived happily enough until the whales started to complain.

'The sea is too crowded as the mermaids are everywhere! The babies play hide-and-seek between our teeth and the teens hitch rides on our fins!' their spokesperson moaned to King Aquidon.

'I will deal with it,' he replied, with a look of concern in his eyes. And he did by moving the mermaids further away from the whales . . . and right into their feeding grounds.

'This will never do! We must go to Aquidon, he'll sort it out!' cried an angry mother whale. Her baby was hungry because she hadn't been able to feed properly as the mermaids were in the way.

As they swam to the palace they secretly wondered whether or not he would listen to them.

They were greeted warmly and Aquidon did listen. He drew a deep breath and told them, 'Whales, I have come to the conclusion that the sea is no longer big enough for us both. One of us must leave and it must be us. We will only return when we can live side by side with enough room to stretch our fins.'

With that the mermaids formed a silent group and disappeared into the ocean. Since then the whales have been calling the mermaids back, begging for forgiveness . . . and that is why whales sing.

Shaffi Batchelor (12)
Bishop Challoner RC Upper School, London

ANYTHING IS POSSIBLE

My body was jelly. This day had come too soon.

The cooking contest was unforgettable and I can still smell the perfumed air, feel myself walking upon the shiny, polished floor. My heart hammered beneath my rib cage. My mind was a tangle of last minute questions, but no answers!

'Next candidate, Delia Smith!'

The audience clapped as I wobbled nervously towards the stage, tripping and stumbling.

'H-hello, I-I'm Delia, a-and I'm g-going to m-make t-tomato s-soup, l-lamb curry with r-rice a-and a chocolate m-mousse.'

It was as if the reason they were there was to wait for you to make mistakes! I made lots of them and after what seemed like a thousand years, I'd produced water with tomato bits in, raw lamb with burnt rice and chocolate 'milkshake'. I could see all the judges writing down each word meaning *failure*.

'Unappetising food, disgusting!'

My mother couldn't look at me with her tear-swamped eyes. Woefully I ran back to her, fighting back the tears. I could feel my heart crumble.

* * * *

'I'll get the post!'

I picked the letter up. *To Delia Smith.* I recognised it immediately and tore open the letter. My eyes fell on the word 'passed'. I stayed silent for a moment, hardly believing it. There was something else in the envelope too. I slid it out and starting reading the first page . . . 'Obviously nervous but I know when a girl has prepared greatly for a contest, and this one had.' I broke into a warm smile.

Alice Chen (12)
Bishop Challoner RC Upper School, London

THE MYTH OF THE DORA

Long before there were stars and a sun in the sky, the world was a very gloomy place . . .

Jonathan, a small village boy, was walking home from an hour's hunting in the woods. As always, he was shivering from the frost which wafted through the air but that wasn't the only reason, it was also pitch-black, so on he went with only rags on his back to keep him warm, all the way home.

Somehow he had managed to take the long way home, therefore finding himself lost. He stopped for a moment and sat down trying to locate where he was. He rose abruptly as he caught a glimpse of something shimmering in a bush; he approached with caution and slowly reached his quivering arm out.

It was a small yet heavy box, wrapped in a soft velvet material. On it was embroidered the following phrase, 'The Dora will only be released to those worthy of its content.'

Jonathan was amazed and even though he hadn't the faintest idea what the phrase meant, he was willing to find out, so he unravelled the box and peeked inside. Suddenly he was pushed back onto the gravel path and a huge light and warmth swept over his body. Warmth he had never experienced in his life.

Because of this little boy's curiosity, he has given the greatest gift to the world, the Dora of light and warmth.

Giselle Villanueva (12)
Bishop Challoner RC Upper School, London

KILLED!

On the 30th September, Mr M Gillerd was killed in a shark attack which was terrifying for family and friends. We found him in hospital (whilst he was still alive). He said, 'I was on a boat ride with my mum, dad and older brother Leon. We were having a great time when suddenly a shark came and tipped the boat and I fell in, but my family were still on-board. I saw a fin, so I swam and swam until I heard a pop as the shark took my leg. I was so scared and now they're just getting me a wheelchair'. Then he unfortunately died.

Mr M Gillerd was eighteen years old and engaged to Miss Sue Ruth.

The wedding has been cancelled due to this tragedy.

Because of this accident the beach where it occurred will be closed all summer.

Jamie Menditta (11)
Blenheim High School, Epsom

HOW THE MANX CAT LOST HER TAIL

Noah was calling the animals to the Ark but there was one cat who was out catching mice and ignored his calls. She was a good mouser but this time she was finding it hard to catch one. She was determined to take a mouse into the Ark with her.

At last, when all the animals were safe in the Ark, the rain began to fall but there was no sign of the cat.
'Who's out is out and who's in is in!' Noah quoted.

With that he started to close the doors, when suddenly the cat, half drowned (this is why cats hate water), tried to squeeze through the gap, but Noah slammed the door on her tail and cut it off.

This is why to this day, the Manx cat does not have a tail.

The cat said:
>'Be bo bend it,
>My tail has ended,
>And I'll go to Man
>And get copper nails
>And mend it.'

Alice Fenner (11)
Blenheim High School, Epsom

SHAPES IN THE SAND

As I followed the winding path over the cliffs, I tried to stifle a sob. What I was doing was wrong and believe me, I knew. However, sometimes we all have to do things we don't want to do, no matter who we will hurt.

The ruby rays of light fingered through my hair and a gentle breeze pushed me towards the sea. The silence of the land roared in my ears, crushing me inside. I stroked the blade in my hand carefully, wishing the end was here and yet wishing it not to come.

Finally I was on the sand, walking towards the gentle, rolling waves. It was almost time . . . and then everything stopped.

The wind ceased blowing and the waves stopped rolling. A mist fell upon me and suddenly I could hear a horse, crying in pain. I searched about myself and then I saw the sands about me come together with a crash.

In their place stood a unicorn, its pearly coat shining brilliantly in the sun. *Of course!* I thought, I had fallen into a dream and I shook myself wildly, trying to wake from my slumber. Nothing changed and I found myself being drawn towards the creature, driven by its beauty.

I tentatively reached out to stroke its mane, but when I brought back my hand, it was covered in blood. I shivered and looked back to the beast but it had disappeared. The world came back into play and the shapes in the sand were over.

Kayleigh Dray (14)
Blenheim High School, Epsom

BARRY ROTTER

The boy who did.

Mr Bernard Jersey was driving to work as normal when a cat suddenly ran into the middle of the road. Unfortunately for the cat Mr Jersey didn't see it until he was on top of it.

He screeched to a halt and went to have a look. The cat lay there looking very dead indeed. Now Mr Jersey was a very cowardly man and not wanting to be blamed for the death of the cat, got an old oil rag from the car, used it to pick up the cat and put the poor creature on the kerb and promptly drove off.
However the cat got up, muttered, 'Flaming Buggles!' and stalked off.

That evening when Mr Jersey arrived home he was sure he saw the same cat he ran over that morning, sitting on his garden wall. 'Coincidence!' he muttered.

That night, on the stroke of midnight, something strange happened - an old man fell out of the sky and landed next to the cat. He picked himself up and sat down next to the cat. 'Why hello, what's your name again?'
'Hello Bumbelbore, remember me, Prof McGonagen.'
'Oh yes, hello Minnie, how are you?'
'Fine! Now Talbus, about the child, where is . . .'
'Did you have a good day?'
'*No!* I was run over by a Buggle again.'
'Well, if you do choose to be a cat, what do you expect?'
'Hmph! Well where is the boy?'
'Badwig's bringing him.'
'What!'

Suddenly they both heard a squeaking sound and a tiny man about three feet high came riding up the street on a tricycle. 'Evenin' Professors!'
'Evening Badwig, have you the child?'
'Yes!'
Badwig produced a small bundle and placed it on the porch mat of the Jersey household.

'Well, that's it then!' said McGonagen.

'Yes . . . no! Not really! We will see him again soon,' said Bumblebore patting McGonagen on the shoulder reassuringly, 'He is the boy who did!'
'Did what?' chorused Badwig and McGonagen.
'I . . . don't really know!'

Daniel Orton (12)
Blenheim High School, Epsom

WHAT IT WAS LIKE TO LIVE IN BRITAIN DURING WORLD WAR II

In this piece of work I will be explaining what it was like to live during World War II.

Evacuation:

Evacuation was for women and children. They were moved and sometimes only the children were evacuated. No children were lost during this evacuation. 38,000 children never saw their parents or brothers and sisters again. The third evacuation took place in 1944 when London was attacked by missiles.

Blitz:

During the war the enemy bombed and killed nearly 40,000 people and destroyed 2,000,000 homes. London was hit the hardest. It was hit 56 nights in a row (which was nearly two months).

Rationing:

Rationing meant a person was allocated a certain amount of food each week. The Government gave everyone a ration book so that the shopkeepers could keep check that it was fair. Exotic fruits were not even tasted until after World War II.

Air Raid Warden:

Air Raid Wardens told people what to do when the siren sounded. You had to take your gas mask and hurry down to the nearest shelter. When the train stopped, it became the bomb shelter.

Crystal Set:

The crystal set was made of older pieces and re-assembled. It was put into some sort of order. It was known as the first radio and it cost about fifty pounds.

Anderson Shelter:

This was a big hole in the ground made from corrugated iron. If you did have one you put suitcases in your house so that when the roof fell in - it fell on the suitcases.

Call-Up Papers:

Call-up papers were sent to young men and women who needed to go and fight for their country.

Home Guard:

The Home Guard were people who were too old or in a reserved occupation. Ex bank managers who were needed at home and their job was to defend this country in case we were invaded. The Home Guard were responsible for the 'black-out'.

Boy's Own Paper:

The young boys' own paper. They even went to work on the fields when they were given away.

It was really hard for people who lived during World War II.

Tanaka Samkange (12)
Blenheim High School, Epsom

THESEUS: INSIDE THE LABYRINTH

As the door clanged shut behind them, Theseus and his companions listened to the echo.

They were trapped inside the labyrinth. Bidding them farewell and assuring them that they would soon be free, Theseus set off alone.

As his eyes adjusted to the dark, Theseus smelt rotting human flesh and the smell of death. He walked slowly through the dark twisting passages, he tasted the human flesh, not by eating but by the smell. He came to a place where the corridor branched in three as he got nearer he heard heavy breathing and a disgusting smell. There, asleep over a human chest, was the Minotaur, its golden horns sharp as daggers and its white nostrils big as craters. He recoiled in horror at the beast. The Minotaur woke as the light of the crown hit his hideous face.

Remembering Ariadne's advice Theseus grasped the dagger in his right hand poised to attack the Minotaur . . .

Charles Oakes (12)
Dedworth Middle School, Windsor

IN THE LABYRINTH

As the door clanged shut behind them, Theseus and his companions listened to the ghostly echo. They were trapped inside the labyrinth. Bidding them farewell and assuring them they would soon be free, Theseus set off alone.

As his eyes were still adjusting to the darkness, Theseus noticed a grotesque stench of stale blood that he could almost taste. The smell of rotting flesh filled his nostrils and his insides turned to liquid. Buckling back at this uninvited smell, Theseus adjusted his focus on the tunnel's long, looming shadows seemed to go on forever, and the ever-twisting labyrinth was pitch-black. The stone walls glistened wet in the light of the crown. Theseus touched the walls but recoiled in horror. They were as cold as the dead, and slimy.

Hours later, Theseus realised he was getting closer. The endless sound of bones crunching and rattling underneath his feet nearly drove him mad, but he thought of his father, and braced himself for what was to come.

Then at last, as he was about to give up, Theseus rounded a corner and found the hideous, ugly Minotaur sleeping over a human chest. Remembering Ariadne's advice, Theseus grabbed the dagger in his right hand poised to attack . . .

Sally Poundall (11)
Dedworth Middle School, Windsor

INSIDE THE LABYRINTH

As the door clanged shut behind them, Theseus and his companions listened to the echo.

They were trapped inside the labyrinth, bidding them farewell and assuring them they would soon be free, Theseus set off alone.

As he walked down the passage, Theseus could smell death in the air. When his eyes adjusted to the dark, he could see outlines of bones on the bloodstained floor.

The walls were ice-cold and slimy as they guided him down the passage. There was an echo of his footsteps all around. Without warning the air began to reek. Theseus could hear heavy breathing around the corner.

In front of him the corridor branched into three. In one of them the Minotaur lay fast asleep, on top of a human chest. Awoken by a dazzle, the Minotaur let out a bellowing roar, so loud that it rocked the ships in the harbour.

His blood-shot eyes stared at Theseus. Fire and smoke were bulging from his nostrils. Then like a bullet train, he started charging.

Remembering Ariadne's warning and advice, Theseus grasped the dagger in his hand, poised to attack the Minotaur!

Joshua Lovell (11)
Dedworth Middle School, Windsor

READY... STEADY... GO!

It was sports day at Layful Manor School for boys. It was a hot, sunny day and I was running in the 70m sprint.

In the race there was me (Chris), Dan, Elliot and Paul . . . Paul the bully, the Minotaur, the monster. In Paul's last race he had hit two boys, breaking one's nose and the other ended up in hospital. I was running in the same race as Paul, I don't know about you but I don't want to end up in a coma. How could I get out of it, I couldn't, I would just have to pray.

'All the runners for the 70m sprint please go to the starting line,' said the commentator.
I slowly went up to the starting line. What! He was next to me. Right! There was no chance, I would die! *Chris Mills died at the age of 13 due to attack, from brutal monster,* it would read on my gravestone. I stood next to Paul wobbling like a jelly.
Then he looked at me and said, 'You don't stand a chance,' and then he laughed.
I gulped. *Help!* I would spend my last day at school, it couldn't get any worse.
The commentator stood up and said, *'Ready... steady... go!'*

George Barlow (11)
Dedworth Middle School, Windsor

BEACH BETRAYAL

In a smart house on the Caribbean coast there lived a smart and sophisticated family. The father, Richard Sheltman was tall, handsome, had brilliant hazel eyes and wavy, golden hair. He was the founder of a small company that made computer programs. His wife, Emily, had previously gone missing during an unfortunate surfing accident and was never seen again. This was an empty space in his life that was growing and could never be replaced. He also had pretty twin daughters, Amy who was clever, good company and loyal to almost everyone. Lori was cunning and had a sharp attitude.

Their neighbours, the Jonstones, were always cheerful and happy to whomever they met. Jeff and Joan were unnaturally cheerful and polite every waking moment! They both worked on a TV chat show called 'Jonstone'. They had two sons, Cameron and Mike, who were polite and ashamed of their parents. They also had a secret. Locked away in their attic was a small fortune of two million, however they never spoke of it to anyone in fact, and they sometimes forgot about it, they had never dipped in it once.

Both Amy and Lori were embarrassed by their soft, sensitive father, they wanted a large, manly figure, not a soft, weeping fluff (as they often referred to him). Their only chance was this, changing his will, because he had left everything to his wife, who was now gone.

So, on a stifling hot day (when he was hot and bothered) they sat down and flew off into very deep and emotional conversation, but they soon became impatient and got to the point quickly.
'Father, what have you left us?' Amy squeaked.
Richard looked flushed and uncomfortable at this statement. 'W-w-well, you know I have left everything to your mother, of course.'
'But she's gone Father, can't you see it?'
'No, she hasn't! She's coming back, she's coming back!'
'Father, I think she's gone. For better or for worse.'
'I'm afraid, I won't change my will. It's getting late. We best be off to bed now, eh?'

Meanwhile, in the Jonstone household their two sons had just discovered the exact same thing in their father's will. They knew of their wealth, *so why not share it out?* they thought. So, they devised a plan to commit matricide in a diary Cameron had been given for Christmas. A fatal mistake.

By this time Amy and Lori were furious with their father, he had given them everything they ever wanted, but not this time. They had become aware that this would not be easy for them and that they would have to persuade him in another fashion. They confided in Cameron and Mike. They told each other of the complete cheek! How dare they! Then Lori had a plan.

A week later when Richard, Jeff and Joan were watching TV at the Sheltmans, they all heard a loud *clunk* come from the kitchen. Joan and Richard went to investigate, but Jeff was hardly frightened. As they went down the hall to the kitchen, four hooded figures jumped out on them. They fell to the floor as their four seven-year-olds drove sharp knives into their backs, crying.

Daniel Hamman (12)
Esher CE High School, Esher

LIZARD CRAZY

There was a boy who lived in California called Sam. Sam was one of those kids who never got phone calls, and always got picked last as sports, he was a loner!

He wore basically the same things geeks always wear, like glasses, a neat and tidy combed-over hairstyle, a red and white T-shirt always tucked in and a supply of pens in his T-shirt pocket and cord trousers. Looking like that it's no wonder he was a loner!

Like every geek in primary school, he had a crush on the most popular girl in school. It's the usual scenario, geek fancied popular girl, geek tried to impress popular girl but popular girl didn't even know he was alive.

To everyone Sam was more boring than a librarian doing a sponsored silence, except for one thing, which was his obsession for lizards, yes lizards. He liked all types of lizards, green ones, red ones, spotty ones, small ones, big ones, massive ones, multicoloured mutated ones, you name it, he liked it. Some would say that made him an even bigger freak if that's possible! He sat for hours with his $5 chemistry set hoping to make a discovery, which just added to his weirdness.

It was Monday, Sam's favourite day of the week because it meant there was a whole week of school and homework and extra homework ahead of him.

It was break.
'Hey look, it's lizard boy,' said Mike Hays, the popular jock.
'Hey lizard boy, did you get a face transplant with one of your lizards?' one of Mike's friends teased.

Sam walked up to Kate, the popular girl, Sam had something behind his back which certainly wasn't a good surprise! 'K-K-Kate.'
'Oh, it's you! I thought it was someone worth turning around for, I was obviously wrong.'
Sam took a long breath in his asthma inhaler. 'W-w-want to see what I've got?'
'What could you possibly have that could interest me?'

Sam put his hand out from behind his back where a slimy lizard crawled across his hand and jumped onto her face and into her mouth.
'Arrgghh!' screamed Kate.
'Oops, sorry!' said Sam.

Kate spat out the lizard which landed into Mrs Khan's coffee. 'You're sorry! A slimy, wet . . . thing that crawls just went into my mouth and you're sorry. Just get away from me freak!' and she walked away.
'Call me!' shouted Sam across the playground.
'In your dreams,' Kate shouted back.
'Every night!' Sam whispered.
'Who put a leaf in my coffee? Wait a minute, that's a . . . a . . . argh! Lizard!'

The next day, after school, there was a knock at the door.
'Hi, I'm Kate's mum, you must be . . . freak at school,' (she read off a piece of a paper).
'I guess so,' said Sam, 'what's that in your hand?'
'Oh, silly me, this is the reason I came, it's a lizard!'
It was, but Sam hadn't seen anything like it. It was pink and purple with a green line down the middle of it. Sam was getting quite excited, he started to pant which Kate's mum obviously found weird.
'I found it at home, I don't know what it was doing there. Oh I just remembered I have to pick my son up from his karate lessons I totally forgot, bye.'

Sam took it up to his room to study it. He started to poke it with a plastic stick that came with his chemistry set.
'Ow, get off me freak,' said the lizard.
Sam jumped out of his chair and got his asthma inhaler. 'I've got an inhaler, and I'm not afraid to use it!'
'Give it a rest lizard boy. Hey does my hair look alright?' said the lizard.
'You're a lizard, you don't have hair,' said Sam a bit shakily.
'What a sad life they must live!' said the lizard.
'Kate, is that you?'
'Like der!'
'Wow, I always knew you'd come into my room one day, it's a matter of probability.'

'Do I look like I care? Anyway can you help me or not?'
'What, help you change back?'
'No, I want you to help me do my homework,' Kate said sarcastically.
'I can if you like.'
'No loser, I was being sarcastic.'
'Oh,' said Sam.
'Let's get on with it, this cage stinks! Oh no wait, I think it's your house!'
'That's my bathroom, the toilet's been blocked for 2 years.'
'Gross!' said Kate.
'This is it, the medicine.'
'Here goes.'

Kate drank it and grew until she was human again. 'Wow! Thanks, I owe you one lizard boy.' She ran out leaving Sam smiling.

There was a knock at the door, it was Principal Scroll with a lizard in his hand.
'Psst, Sam, it's me, Mrs Khans!'
'Oh no!' Sam said quietly. He looked outside and saw hundreds even thousands of lizards in his front garden. 'Noooo!' he shouted.

Daryl Rogers (13)
Esher CE High School, Esher

THE SUN

On the 4th January a crime was committed by the most sinister, evil, dark and unusual man. A man by the name of Shelter.

Shelter has a dark past and an even deeper future.

The charge for this particular behaviour is *life in the box!* Shelter has remained anonymous to his victims.

He describes himself as very upper, strongly built and an ex-army recruit.

Before he claimed his victims he used to say that there was a shelter down the road, a new one. He could help.

He gave them food and drink and gave them a bath, and as they fell asleep, they never awoke.

Now he has killed 8 people, all homeless. This happens near the height of darkness when they are cold. To all those that have lost the homeless members of their families, God bless you and your loved ones up above in the clouds.

If you see any strange activity from a man, call our hotline 0800 321 123. Thank you!

Kerry Scotney (12)
Glenthorne High School, Sutton

THE PATH OF LIFE

One day in the future I am going to be a multi-millionaire with a huge house and a bed made out of £50 notes, with an unlimited supply of food and drink but that will never happen now because I am a homeless bum with no friends. If I remember rightly my name is Tom and I am 23 years old.

I haven't got any cash except when I sell the Big Issue every now and then. Sometimes I get so desperate I rob shops. Once I even thought about getting into jail, at least then I would get a bed, food and clothes.

People walking past make me jealous of their families. One day I even thought I saw my dad, he came over and dug in his pocket and said, 'God bless you, you poor man,' and walked off, that's what made me go back.

I walked for miles but when I got there, hesitated and knocked on the door. A young boy answered, I wondered whether he was my brother or just a boy, a middle-aged woman walked to the door and burst into tears, it was my mum. I was so happy, she invited me in for a cup of tea and to catch up on old things. It was great, I had a lovely meal, I really thought I was that millionaire, I dreamt of being. That night I went to bed in a nice warm bed. That's where I am now, goodnight.

Richard Sheehan (13)
Glenthorne High School, Sutton

SUPER SPY SAVES SUTTON!

Magnificent super spy saves the town of Sutton.

The spy that has been working on catching the evil Dr E X Plosive has finally got him.

This super spy would not give us his name but we are trying to work on it, however if someone might know what his name is, they are more than welcome to mention it to us!

Apparently this evil Dr has been trying to take over the world for 15 years but his plans have been ruined due to things like war and lack of experience for his seventy-five-year-old soldiers.

The police have been looking for him ever since he decided to blow up Big Ben but then realised his secret underground lair was right underneath!

Dr E X Plosive has moved to places like St Paul's Cathedral, Buckingham Palace, the London Eye and the bin behind the Glenthorne High School's canteen! Obviously he was a bit loopy!

If you have heard anything about the evil Dr or even the secret spy then please call us on this number: 0800-I-know-something-about-the-super-spy.

Terry Angell (13)
Glenthorne High School, Sutton

SCREAM!

There is an old house on Portibelo Street. No one dared go near it. It is a very old house and most of the windows are boarded up. The garden is overgrown, as it hasn't been touched in years, and . . . most scary, it is believed to be haunted with the most horrible ghosts. No one has ever survived once they had entered. Some people say that on a full moon, during the midnight hours, you can hear a high-pitched scream coming from the house.

'Go on! I agree with Joe, I think we should do something more interesting around here, why not.'
'Fred! The place is haunted! Everyone that's gone in there has died! I don't fancy suicide today! Besides, it's not that boring around here,' Sam said.
'Come on . . . wimp! Well me and Fred'll go without you then,' Joe said, hoping for Sam to change his mind.
There was a long pause.
'OK, I'll go. God!' Sam sighed, 'I can't believe you persuaded me to actually go in that house . . . at night! Ah man!'

The next night, the three blond teenagers snuck out and met at the house at 11pm. Once they were all there, they agreed to go in.

They struggled to get through the overgrown garden, to get to the door. The door creaked as they opened it cautiously. The three of them looked in with horror. The last that was heard of the foolish teenagers, was their screams.

David Mew (13)
Glenthorne High School, Sutton

A Day In The Life Of Anna-Louise

Hello, my name is Anna-Louise and I am nine years of age. I was born on the fourth of March 1930. My mum has sent us away and we haven't seen Father for ages. He went away to fight for our country against Germany but I am scared he might die. My mother tells me not to be so ridiculous but I can tell that she is worried too. She has sent my little brother Benjamin and me to a foster home by ourselves. She says it is for the best, but I want to see her and I am missing her terribly.

We are on the train now and Benny is scared, but we are nearly there. There are many other children on the train and I find myself looking around and wondering if I will be sharing a home with them. I've spotted some children that I think look quite nice but then I go back to thinking about Mother and Father. Benny has caught me crying and asked me why I was. I mumbled something about dust in my eye and because he is only four he was convinced.

We are finally here, at the home and it is enormous. The people are lovely too but I still have my parents on my mind. We have had time to unpack and we have also had dinner. It is time for bed now and I shall pray for my family. Goodnight.

Laura Bessick (12)
Harris City Technology College, London

BEYOND THE FOREST OF MACCOBE

The Forest of Maccobe is a mystical, wondrous place. The Forest of Maccobe has the widest range of any animal that could be imagined by a young child. Many people who venture within the Forest of Maccobe never return. Some people started small villages but the weak people, they simply ceased to exist. And it's not just weak people who disappear. Strong, bombastic people often fall prey to the forest, for you see no matter how strong you are, the forest is stronger. No matter how quick you are, the forest is quicker. And no matter how smart you are, the Forest of Maccobe is always smarter.

The Bad Weather Five were the first people to try and stand up against the forest. They each came from the same village and could each summon an element of their own. The Hawk could summon wind, Shinzo could summon water, Twig summoned fire, Geo-dude summoned earth and The Summoner, who was the leader of the group, could control gravity, which I understand isn't an element but he likes to think it is. The Bad Weather Five left their village in search of an answer to the question; is there more out there? They wanted to know if they could go beyond what they thought was the ultimate force in the universe and despite all odds, they did.

What they found was amazing. It was so flabbergasting that on the way back they were not prepared for the forest's deep underbelly, which they had narrowly passed through before. Only one made it back to tell the tale of what they had seen. And it was that adventure that inspired so many people of all ages to set out, and try and go beyond the Forest of Maccobe.

Aaron Hamilton (11)
Harris City Technology College, London

TAKEARRA

Near a town, lived an ordinary teenager. Maybe this sounds unusual but an ordinary teenager? There's no such thing. Takearra was always going into town with her best mate but there was one thing that she hid from everyone.

One night, Takearra and Sherrece went into town. They walked up Syllabi Way and around the corner to the bus garage. 10 minutes later a bus came and they laughed and told jokes on their way. They had a great time at PHD club and were now on their way home. Takearra had to get the 430 but Sherrece had to get the 292. Takearra decided to get the 292 as she didn't want to go home on her own.

Takearra got off the bus and Sherrece offered to walk with her but she said that she would be fine. She walked down Garratage Road but never made it down Ferlannie Road. Someone or something grabbed her as she tripped over a little rock on the road.

Sherrece had phoned to see if Takearra had got home alright but she wasn't home. Her mum was really worried.

An hour later Takearra came home and her mum was fussing over her. Takearra told a lie as she just said that she went to see Mr Braining on Lever Road. She told this lie because the person or thing had said if she told anyone what had happened, they would kill her.

The next year, Takearra reported it to Tavenmay police station.

Dion Arthur (11)
Harris City Technology College, London

A Day In The Life Of A Teacher!

'Hello Diane, how are you? I was also wondering what items were going to be raffled today. I quite fancied that personal music player,' questioned Mrs Lamb as she entered the staffroom.
'Oh I'm fine, but no, I don't know what's going to be raffled today. But I do think it's a marvellous idea to raffle the items we have confiscated from the children,' replied Miss Hodds.

The bell had just rung and Mrs Lamb and Miss Hodds were in a deep discussion about the great pleasure they received when they hand out detentions. Also, when they make pupils redo their homework in order for a longer time to mark essays etc.

'Sorry I am late girls, I was in an important meeting,' lied Mrs Lamb as she seated herself at her desk. 'I must be going mad saying sorry to the pupils,' Mrs Lamb muttered to herself. 'What was that Rebecca?' demanded Mrs Lamb.
'Oh I was just sayin' to Caroline I saw you comin' out of the staffroom laughin' and that to Miss Hodds,' Rebecca answered.
'Well, as you seem to spend your time seeing me around the school premises perhaps you will enjoy seeing me after school in detention, in B8. I would also like to tell you how unflattering that make-up you're wearing is and since you obviously don't know the school rules I will print you off another copy,' concluded Mrs Lamb, pleased with herself for having company in detention.

'Hello Rebecca, it's good to see you made it to detention. I expect you have some homework with you that needs completing,' muttered Mrs Lamb.
'No, sorry Miss,' murmured Rebecca.
'Oh that's good as I have an essay I would like you to complete and once again it's not Miss it is Mrs Lamb,' reminded Mrs Lamb.
'I'm surprised I wouldn't fink anyone would wanna marry a moaner like you!' whispered Rebecca.
'Although I hate a child who is rude I have ensured I have company for the next four detentions I shall be doing and I will expect no talking, eating, rudeness or questions,' shouted Mrs Lamb after she had opened a packet of crisps.

'You know I was a bit worried about yesterday's detention, you'll be relieved I did find someone to keep me company,' said Mrs Lamb to Miss Hodds.

'Good morning class and Mary please take out those earrings,' yelled Mrs Lamb.

'But Mrs Lamb, it said in the school rules we are allowed to wear a bit of jewellery,' replied Mary.

'Yes, but what you're wearing is a monstrosity, not jewellery and if you know what the school rules say about holding doors for your peers and elders, you will not mind spending your break holding the school's main doors open!'

That same day Mrs Lamb walked through the school's main doors with a smug face, guess who was holding the doors?

Georgia Colville (12)
Maidstone Grammar School For Girls, Maidstone

BENCHY, THE OVER-ENTHUSIASTIC HEDGEHOG

Benchy was a hedgehog from under the bush. He was mischievous and disobedient and always answered back. But today, Benchy had an adventure that would always be remembered, a hard and horrible lesson. And from that day on, Benchy would never be disobedient again.

It was a bright autumn morning. Benchy wriggled and crawled out of his dry-leafed bed. He felt adventurous and excited, so he persuaded his sister Bristles to join him in the sun for a game of hide-and-seek.

'Benchy, you know we 'ent s'posed to, dere's cats an ev'rythink up dere, we shood wait for Mum.'
'Bristles, 'ave you evar seen a cat?'
'No, but you nevar no, one cood spring on us any minit.'
'Come *on* Bristles, nuthinks gonna happen.'
'Fine, but if anythink does happen . . .'
'Yes, yes, I'm responsible, now get out dere.'

Bristles peered cautiously out of the hole and with a prompting nudge from Benchy, scrabbled out. Benchy didn't even look left or right as he bounded out the hole and landed, sprawling playfully on the grass below.

'Right,' said Benchy, almost jumping with anticipation, 'you count and I'll 'ide, only not too far away from the hole OK?' and off he scrambled before Bristles could complain.

Bristles gave a large grumble and settled on the grass counting peacefully to fifty. Meanwhile, Benchy had settled behind a long tug of weeds and was trembling with excitement. But poor Benchy didn't notice the cat! She had crept up and now with a large hiss, sprang upon the hedgehog. But Benchy heard the hiss and curling into a ball, he rolled away as fast as he could. Bristles heard the thud as cat met earth and spun around as quick as a whip to see her dear brother rolling away with a cat pouncing desperately but always missing by an inch.

Meanwhile, Benchy wasn't conscious of Bristles yelling his name as loud as thunder, only of getting away and getting away fast. Suddenly, Benchy noticed a large hump right in his way. It was too close for him to swerve out of the way and before he knew it there was a tremendous scrape on the back of his neck and he was flying up, up, up and it then went dark as he flew through the door of a shed window in his path.

'Argghh!' screamed Benchy as he landed, (just missing the floor) into a pile of sawdust.

Meanwhile Bristles was running as fast as her feet could carry her to the shed, taking care not to go the same way as the cat did. She squeezed her nose through the crack that she found and whispered urgently, 'Benchy, oh Benchy, are you OK? Oh Benchy where are you?'

'Mime mire!' yelled Benchy, trying in vain to spit sawdust out of his mouth.

'Shhh! Benchy not so loud, vat cat's still out dere. Look, I'll go tell Mum where you are, god shill be worrid sick.'

'No! Oh god no, pleese don't leave me 'ere alone Bristles, I'm scared!'

'I 'ave to Benchy, look we'll come back strate away and we'll rescue you, I promise!'

As Bristles scampered away, Benchy shivered and reluctantly dragged himself away from the sawdust and stared gloomily at his surroundings. The shed was dusty and cobwebby and smeared with mud.

Then there came a scrabbling that disturbed the silence and made Benchy jump like anything and a mouse sprang out of the sawdust.

'Who are you?' came the curt voice of the mouse, 'and what are you doing here?'

'My name is Benchy,' answered the trembling hedgehog, 'and I was chased in here by the cat.'

The mouse mumbled to himself and then asked, 'Do you wish to get out again?'

'Why yes, of corse, why, cood you pleese 'elp me?'

The mouse gave him a piercing look, 'I could,' he murmured quietly, 'I could . . .'

'Oh then pleese, 'elp me!'

The mouse smiled, 'Yes, I shall Benchy.' And with that, he turned around and whistled, a shrill whistle that made Benchy cringe. At his command, there came a dozen spiders and to them the mouse commanded, 'Fit this hedgehog with a safety harness and attach a rope

to the ceiling. He must be ready to both swing back through the window and land safely on the grass by tonight.'
And the spiders scattered off to do their jobs.

'He did *what?'* bellowed Shriga, Bristles mother. 'What, just flew into the shed?'
'Yeh Mum, but he's dead cold an' fritand an' I promised that I wood return so *come on Mum.'*

Bristles nudged her mother out the hole and ran to the shed, noting that the cat had gone. Bristles thought that her mother was so upset; she would knock the whole house down with the fear for her son. As soon as they got to the shed, Shriga poked her nose through the door and boomed, *'Benchy!* Oh Benchy, sweetie, are you alright?'
'Yeh Mum!' came the faint reply, 'Harry's gonna fix me up with a spider silk harness.'
'Harry, who's Harry?'
'This mouse who lives 'ere.'
'Spider silk harness?'
'Yeh Mum, he's lord of the spiders, an' he's gonna swing me through da window.'
'Hmmm . . . well, I'm not happy about this swinging through the window. Isn't there another option?'
'Yeh Mum, I cood starve to death while waiting for the humans to open the door.'
'OK sweetie. Erm . . . when will you be out?'
'Tonight at the latest Mum,' answered Benchy after a brief pause.
'Well . . . hurry up.'

Harry's invention wasn't complex, but it worked well. It consisted of him holding one end of a long and thick piece of silk. This silk travelled over the beam at the top and back under to where Benchy was harnessed. The harness wrapped around the hedgehog's belly and he was quite safe. Harry had to work quickly. He had to fire Benchy through the window and with the help of some spiders, let the rope out so that he could touch the ground safely. It would be hard, but he was ready.

On the other end of the harness stood Benchy, who could make no sense of this apparatus. He was nervous. Outside stood Bristles and her mother with a spider so that they knew exactly what was happening. They weren't saying much. They were nervous.

Suddenly Benchy took off. As if in slow motion, Harry pulled and then loosened the rope and Benchy sailed down into his mother's clutching arms.
'I'll never do it again Mum, I promise.' And all three of them trotted to their nice, warm hole under the hedge.

Emily Hogan (12)
Maidstone Grammar School For Girls, Maidstone

A Day In The Life Of Abu, A Thai Elephant

The sun rose over the canopy of the treetops for the start of a new day. It was going to be a hot one and it was already humid. The monkeys were chatting as usual, the little ones racing through the branches calling teasingly for each other. Insects and birds joined in chorus and the Mahoûts started to awaken the herd.

Crunching on a breakfast of foliage, I tenderly placed my trunk over the shoulder of my Mahoût knowing he had a supply of tiny Thai bananas. Flapping my ears to keep cool, I enjoyed our quiet moments together.

Not long after, the Mahoûts were calling the herd to start the trek up to the jungle. It was a long walk but finally we reached the top. Now the work began to get even more tiring. The already chopped logs were tied to the chains that were wrapped around our bodies, across our shoulders, around our necks and draped down our backs. They were heavy and although we have tough skin they rubbed against it making it very sore. Luckily my Mahoût is kinder than the rest but still hits me aggressively with a sharp point at the end of a stick to ensure that I carry on working. We've been together for many years now and we have a good relationship, but I know he is worried because gradually all the forests in Thailand will be knocked down for buildings used by humans for work and to live in.

As the humidity gets higher we eventually reach our destination, the chains are untied and we start piling the logs with our trunks. We call to each other ensuring that we are all alright, even though we are very tired with swollen feet.

Our morning work is done and now we are taken to bathe in the river. We love to lie in the cool water and our Mahoût scrubs behind our ears and we tease them, squirting water at them. Monkeys swing through the trees of the camp, being irritating as usual and lizards sunbathe on the rocks.

After bathing we have some free time. I wander among the herd and we think about the time before the Masai elephant camp existed. Of how we used to be taken to Chang Mai City to try and get food from tourists to survive. I hated it, the lights would dazzle me and the honking and screeching of the tuk-tuks and traffic in the road would terrify me. I remember Mahab rampaging through the street, terrified, causing such a commotion, he trampled a human and caused an accident. It was a dreadful night, poor Mahab was destroyed and tourists reported how bad we elephants were. No one understood.

The government banned us from the city and opened the camp. We now live here, working with our Mahoûts and entertaining tourists in the afternoons.

My thoughts return to the present as Abuba, a local Buddhist priest laughs and strokes my trunk. He's brought me sugar cane. He announces the arrival of a coach of tourists and we hear them giggling and sighing at the sight of us.

We like to wander amongst them. They give us bananas and sugar cane and love having their photos taken. My trick is to take the paper Baht money from their back pockets. It tastes lovely and the tourists think it's funny.

I hold Ghani's trunk and a woman sits between our entwined trunks and we swing her while she has her photo taken. It's strange what little things the humans enjoy but we gain lots of food and attention.

I walk towards the gatehouse with my Mahoût. I love kicking a giant ball between my friends. I can kick the furthest, we pass to each other, running, swinging our trunks and . . . I score a goal, the crowd cheers. The ball hits someone's head in the crowd and everyone laughs. My Mahoût beckons me over and I cross my front legs and take a bow. My Mahoût climbs onto my neck and we walk out of the stadium.

The next tricks are my worst nightmare. We all gather in the centre. Our Mahoûts prod us with the spike-back, back, oh! I have trouble with my limbs, but I raise the front of my body - and yes, I can make it. I'm up on my back legs and walk on two like a human. There's murmurs in the crowd and I launch forward. I heave my great body now onto my front legs and produce a handstand. Applause is heard but many mutter that it is cruel. I find it so difficult. My limbs are so tired and sore but this is what the tourists pay for.

Sabu raises his trunk and a cry echoes through the open space as a spike descends on him. He's not very good at these tricks and his Mahoût is cross.

Cameras click and flash for ages. People want to come and pat us but I'm so exhausted and we've still got another trek to do.

I pinch some sugar cane from under the arms of a man, he laughs but it tastes good.

We are led to the ramp where huge seats are strapped by ropes around out necks and middles. It's time to take humans for a ride through the jungle. Two huge men climb into my seat. The weight is incredible. The sun is still hot and they complain of the heat, sweating heavily they say they need drinks.

We start to walk. I look forward to the steep slope where the path is shaded by the trees. We stop as usual as someone in their excitement spots our white elephant in the distance.

My Mahoût commands me to move. Through the jungle we go, stopping now and then I raise my trunk to trumpet to my friends. They joke about my fat men.

The journey is nearly at an end, photos are taken and the men finally get off.

I walk to the shade and we can hear the coaches leaving.

We have a final dip in the river and the sun begins to sink in the sky. We gather by our Mahoûts' huts, it's my favourite part of the day. The jungle is at peace with its own kind. I can rest my weary body for the night before work starts again tomorrow.

Tabitha Duffield (12)
Maidstone Grammar School For Girls, Maidstone

A Day In The Life Of A Bear Who Was Made To Dance

Here I sit, staring up at the stars in the clear blue night sky, my female friend bounds past me, it must be teatime. How can she look so happy? She suffered the same experience as me, maybe mine was worse than hers or maybe she's stronger than me. Even though it's my favourite tea, a variety of fruit and vegetables, (now Bella, my so-called friend, will take all the nicest apples, but anyway) I will sit here and tell you my story, so you are aware of what's going on and you are able to do something about it . . .

I'm a big brown bear with claws like huge metal nails and teeth like tusks of an elephant, scary, you might be thinking. I wouldn't even threaten to harm an ant let alone a human, I'm a big softie on the inside! From the moment I was born into this world I knew something was wrong. I wasn't born in a jungle or forest, in my natural environment, among trees, plants and other animals, I was born in a cold, dingy room, snatched from my mother was I, before I could even start to cry. Without my mum I thought I'd have nobody, nobody to cuddle up to when I was cold or scared, nobody to wipe my tears, what would I do?

I managed to grow up with just human company, it was hardly nice company though. I can't think of words to describe it, hell maybe, or torture, they didn't know how to treat me or even feed me. I became very overweight, being fed tons of scraps each day, my huge tummy gave me an awfully sore back and made it hard for me to walk. Each time I think back to the bad times it makes me feel sick and it brings a tear to my eye. As time went on I decided not to eat everything I was given, after a long period my weight improved and I became an incy-wincy bit healthier.

Without exercise each of my limbs ceased up, I was locked in a tiny cage (I couldn't stand up in it, neither could I live) metal bars surrounded me. Either my feet or my bottom always became dreadfully painful because whichever way the cage was turned metal bars were always the bottom floor.

I really must begin to tell you about why all this was happening otherwise I'll miss my bedtime as well as my tea!

One day I remember there being a lot of fuss, the noise of people's voices was unbearable. I started to shake the cage madly, trying to get the people's attention, they all turned to look at me, the room fell silent. I was scared, what should I do? The man who came to see me each day, the one who gave me food and water, came towards me. He was carrying two huge metal chains, with big metal rings on the end. They looked very heavy, he needed two hands to carry them, I remember feeling terrified, anxious to know what was going on.

Cutting a very long story short, those chains were for me. I tried to show the people that I didn't want them, but they didn't take any notice. My owner attached each one around my waist, carelessly he caught my fur and even my skin once or twice. The best thing though was being free from that horrid cage, I was able to walk. I tried to be on my best behaviour, *maybe*, I thought, *they will soon take the chains off and let me be free, free to the world,* that's my dream.

'He's fine, on his best behaviour, let's dress him up,' shouted a man in a very common voice.

Dress who up? I wondered. *Surely not me, that would just be a joke,* I thought. This was not real though, flowers and bells were attached to me and more chains, I felt like a doll being thrown around by a five-year-old.

The thing I'm going to tell you next is the most upsetting thing I've experienced, I even find it hard telling people about it. This was my first taste for bear dancing. I want you to imagine the intense heat, the midday sun is boiling and you have lots of bits and pieces, chains and bells hanging off you. Two men pull you towards a metal plate, you're trying to pull back but the men are stronger than you. The feeling when my first foot hit the plate was unbelievable, indescribable, you may be wondering why? Well, my owners thought if burning metal was placed under my feet I would dance. I had to, I had no chance, I hopped from foot to foot, my owner playing a high-pitched banjo in my ear. My head was spinning, I was confused, also angry and annoyed, they consider this torture and pain to be entertainment?

As days went on my blisters grew bigger and far more painful, on days when I felt stubborn I refused to perform although I got whipped. This caused more pain and made me cry even more though, but I didn't realise this. I performed about six times a day, by the evening I was always exhausted and literally starving and gasping for water. I'm no doctor but I'm sure that I became dehydrated, fainting every so often and having dizzy spells. After some time I was taught many new tricks, people would laugh and clap in my face, people often threw money at me which I had to dodge. None of the money I, and I repeat I made, was spent on me, my owners probably spent it on some jazzy car or mobile phone.

After weeks, days, months or maybe years (I don't know because I lost track of time) came some happy news for me. A well-known charity from England, who deal with cruelty to animals abroad, came to rescue me. This was a dream come true, you may wish to be a princess or maybe a millionaire but my dream was to not have to earn a living for someone else whilst experiencing pain and torture.

Here I am today eating a healthy diet, with a lot of exercise and soon hopefully (touch wood) I will be released to my natural habitat. Though it wasn't an easy journey all the way, it took a lot of people and a lot of tender love and care to get me where I am.

I hope all you people out there are now aware that cruelty to animals goes on all around the world. By supporting charities that help prevent this, you can make a difference. Anyway, I must go as I can only see a couple of apples left and if I don't leave now they will all be gone, bye!

Emily Manners (12)
Maidstone Grammar School For Girls, Maidstone

A Dolphin's Day

I was one year old when it happened. It was a lovely sunny day in the ocean and I was getting a lesson from my mother on how to catch the small fish we eat.

I saw a strange shape and went to take a closer look. I got closer and closer to the shape, suddenly I was caught in something that was pulling me up to the surface. I looked around for my family - I was terrified! I found myself surrounded by fishermen. They looked surprised to find me in their net. Then unusual sounds filled the air - clicking and whistling noises.

The fishermen went to have a look. It was my family coming to find me. I was very happy to see them. The fishermen decided to reunite me with my family.

I was really hungry by now and needed my dinner.

Lilly Daisy Cook (12)
Majorie McClure School, Chislehurst

THE LEGEND OF THE THREE-HEADED LION

Long ago in the heart of Camelot there was a village and in that village there lived a king, a king named King George.

George went out to hunt deer. Seconds later there was an earthquake and a massive creature appeared. This creature looked strange. It had not one, not two but three heads - a head of a lion, a head of a cobra and a head of a dragon. This creature could breathe out fire and a beam of ice. Its name was Licobran.

King George raced back to the village to tell everyone they were in mortal danger. 'Will you go and kill Licobran?' the King asked in a terrifying voice.
'Yes Your Majesty,' said a knight.
The King said, 'If you kill that three-headed beast I will reward you with gold or silver.'
So the knight set off to kill Licobran.

On reaching Licobran's lair he thought about what it would be like to have gold or silver. Something broke his concentration - suddenly a large three-headed creature appeared roaring and following him. Reaching the village the King asked him, 'Have you killed Licobran yet?'
'No Your Majesty,' the knight replied.

Licobran ran rapidly to the village destroying everything standing in its path. The knight pulled out his sword and stuck it in the heart of Licobran. Licobran dropped to the floor, and from that day the knight was known as 'Victorious'.

Mark Alan Seagers (12)
Majorie McClure School, Chislehurst

THE QUEST

I was asked to go and see the king for a mission. I was talking to the king and he said to me that he would give me a quest to go and kill thirty men in a village who had been terrorising the area. I went home and thought about it.

The next day I went back and I said that I would accept the quest. The king said to me that he would reward me with money, gold and a castle if I completed the quest. So I set off to go and kill these men in the village.

I had been travelling for a day when I came across a forest, but not any forest! This forest had trees growing across it so I got out my sword and cut it all down. It took me three days to get through it and I was very tired when I got to the end of the forest. There was a waterfall right at the end so I thought about it and in the end I just jumped. *Splash!* I was at the bottom of the waterfall. I had to swim for a while to get out because all of the sides were high. I got out at last and had to walk through lots of fields, forests and across rivers, but at last I got to the village.

There were men everywhere so I had to think about how I was going to attack them. I thought that I should attack at night.

It got to the night and I grabbed my sword and I ran into the village and there were about ten men walking around. I ran at them, cut them up and left them all dead. Then I ran around to see if there were any more and there must have been at least twenty men. I ran at them again. They were coming at me from all angles. Once I had killed one, another one came along, one after the other, more and more until I came to the last one. He stabbed his sword into my arm, then he punched me in the head again and again.

Out of nowhere I found some energy and got up and jumped for my sword. He ran after me and I turned around and blocked one of his jabs. Then I jumped at him and pinned him on the ground. I got my sword and jammed it into his heart. I got up and left him on the ground dying, blood everywhere.

Now I was injured it would be harder to make the trip back. Blood was running down my arm. I started to go home. I just reached the waterfall and it took me two days to get there and my arm by that time was a mess. I washed it in the river. I waited for the morning and then set off on my journey again.

I couldn't get up the waterfall with my arm so I walked down until the cliff ended.

Three days later I got back to the forest and this time I did not have to cut the trees out of my way.

Three days later I was just out of the forest and now close to home again. It took me about another twenty-four hours to get back home to the castle. I went to the king first thing and everybody was pleased to see me back again. I had a long talk with the king and at the end of it all he gave me a welcome back party as well as a castle, a lot of gold and money. At the end of the night I went home to my castle and already my arm was getting better.

Daniel Slack (13)
Sunnydown School For Boys, Caterham

THE QUEST

I am a knight and the king has asked me to save his daughter from a fire-breathing dragon. The reward, if I do save her, is two hundred shillings and her hand in marriage.

When I was on my way to find her, there was a huge thunderstorm that was blocking my way. It was cutting down all of the trees. I had to get on my noble steed and chop down and jump over the trees.

When I got to the mountain I saw nothing, but just when I was about to leave, a fire-breathing dragon appeared. It was the size of six houses and had the power of thirty knights. It had the same amount of fire as a whole volcano.

I fought and fought, using my shield to defend my body when the beast was using his fire at me. While he was regaining his fire, I went up to him and went under his tummy and stuck the sword right into his heart. The creature died immediately.

I took my newly-wed wife and rode off into the distance. And we lived happily ever after.

Scott Bennett (13)
Sunnydown School For Boys, Caterham

THE QUEST

My world is in danger from a magical ring. It is guarded by a monster. The king asked me to help, so two days later I went on my quest. I went on horseback.

We came across all sorts of tasks. We came to a mountain. I sensed that we were near because I could sense the power of the ring. I was climbing the mountain. My horse went another way around. I saw the big flame of fire which made the rock fall. I ran quickly to the other side. After it was over I saw that it had opened up a little cave. I went to the other side. My horse was waiting for me so I carried on. It took me another three days to get there.

I got to the dragon's lair and I walked in. The dragon was not there. I saw the ring. I ran and grabbed it. I saw these pots that were so big it was amazing.

I suddenly saw a big dragon coming so I climbed in one of the pots. The dragon was carrying some logs. It put them down then breathed fire at the logs so I jumped out. I ran. I saw the dragon was close to me and I was at the edge of a cliff. I stopped but the dragon didn't. When it fell I cut its head off. Then I headed back home.

When I got home there was a big celebration. It went on all day. At the end we destroyed the ring.

Edward Baxter (12)
Sunnydown School For Boys, Caterham

THE QUEST

Once upon a time there was a knight who had powers - they were flying powers and fire powers. He had a big brain and he could run very fast. He had X-ray vision and he was very strong.

A king asked him to rescue his daughter. The reward was her hand in marriage. A monster had kidnapped her and he had to kill the monster.

The monster stuck to the wall and grabbed the knight and froze him, but the knight melted the ice and picked him up and threw him. The knight burnt him with his special powers and he died.

Everyone had a party and the mayor came to it. A week later the knight got married to the king's daughter and lived happily ever after.

Russell Smith (13)
Sunnydown School For Boys, Caterham

THE QUEST

The king said that I was the best knight in the world and the only one courageous enough to do the quest. So I listened carefully as he told me what he wanted me to do. My quest was to find the Holy Grail. I knew this would be very, very hard so the reward was one *billion* pounds. There were a lot of things that I could do with one billion pounds. I decided to accept the quest.

I was travelling for a couple of days but at last I got to a forest. I started to walk through the forest until it got so thick I could not go on any further. I was so tired that I fell asleep.

I had the weirdest dream. It told me to dip my sword into a river. When I woke up I tried it and it worked like a treat. I tried it on a tree and it cut through the tree like paper. The rest of the forest did not hold me back so I was through it in a couple of hours.

I found out where the Holy Grail was but it was guarded by a monster in the top of a castle. As I got near to the top of the castle I saw a load of bones! Suddenly the monster jumped out of nowhere. He looked disgusting.

It had big teeth and big eyes. There were scales all over his body. We started to fight. I went to stab him in the chest but he moved and I ended up stabbing him in the mouth. I was very happy to get one billion pounds to take home. The king was very happy to get the Holy Grail. There was a big celebration for me coming back home.

Ricky Holroyd (12)
Sunnydown School For Boys, Caterham

THE QUEST

I had been commanded to go to the king's court. When I arrived the king gave me a quest; a quest to find his family's long-lost sword. Without the sword the rivers would dry up and the crops would wither and die.

I set off in search of the sword. I had heard news that the sword was in the mountains, so I headed there.

I came across a wood. It was too large to go around so I had to go through it. I found a woodcutter's house and borrowed his axe. I spent days chopping down the trees to make a path. When I got to the other side I continued on with my quest to find the missing sword. I rode on my horse all the way to the mountains, eating fish and sleeping under trees.

When I got to the mountains, I found a cave. I was just about to enter the cave when I heard a roaring sound. I ran and hid behind a rock. A dragon came running out of the cave. Its teeth and claws glistened in the daylight. It scorched the ground with its breath. It turned around and whacked its whip-like tail against one of the other rocks, then went back into the cave.

I waited until nightfall. I could hear the dragon sleeping - its snoring shaking the ground. I sneaked into the cave. I saw the dragon coiled around the sword, sleeping. I pulled the sword out of the ground, the dragon woke up instantly. I stabbed it with the sword. The dragon moved clumsily from side to side, then it fell down dead. I pulled the sword out of it and cleaned the blood off.

Joyfully I rode down the mountain through the fields and forest, back to the king's court. The rivers flowed and the crops grew once more. I was knighted and married to the king's daughter.

Matthew Bartholomew (13)
Sunnydown School For Boys, Caterham

THE QUEST

I, Legalos heard about a queen in trouble. My quest was to help her. The reward was a gold plate and some money. I had been chosen for the quest.

I had to go through a forest and a tree whispered some magic words to me. The tree said to me to say the magic word 'quest'. The wood and I did and a path appeared. Suddenly an Ork tried to kill me so I fired an arrow right in his eye and the Ork died.

Next, I had to face a monster. The monster had a sword, a shield and sharp teeth, but I fought him off. Then another Ork came and I fired another arrow at its eye.

I felt proud and honoured. I had a party and I got my princess and some gold and I lived happily ever after.

Lee Bainbridge (12)
Sunnydown School For Boys, Caterham

A Day In The Life Of David Long

13th May 1349

This morning I woke up with a terrible pain around my armpits and my groin. I woke Ma up who was next to me in bed, along with my 3 brothers and sister. 'Ma,' I screamed in her ear, 'I think I've got the plague!'

Ma jumped out of bed and started examining me straight away. As soon as she saw the lumps on my body she panicked and hurried my family out of the room before examining them too. The other families in our tenement block panicked as well, therefore I got locked in the cellar under the block.

So here I am now in a cellar, with no food or water, not that it's much of a change though. My family is out on the streets at the moment burning my clothes to stop the plague spreading.

These stupid flowers were supposed to keep the plague away! Why did vinegar have to be so expensive? Maybe that would have helped me and why didn't I listen to Josh's advice and throw away that stupid sailor's bone? I guess there's no going back for me now!

I do hope that Elsa won't get the plague, or Tom, Jack, John or Mother, as I love them all dearly. Although I do wish that they would come and see me. Well, the only place that I'm going to see them again is in Heaven. I'll just lie here and wait for God to pick me up and take me there.

Goodnight!

Harriette Salvage (12)
Sutton High School, Sutton

SELF-IMAGE

I strip. The scales loom ahead. I walk towards them as fear creeps through. I step. The dial swings. Thank god it's less than yesterday. I dress and run back to my room. Just four more pounds then things will change. I stare; my body looks the same. In the mirror a fat girl is staring back.

My mind wanders. The fridge is full of food. It's all there waiting for another binge. I run. I can hear the food calling. I fill my mouth again and again, chocolate, crisps, bread, anything I can find. I remember. I spit into the sink, retching and retching. Get it out! Get it out! Back to the scales and once again the night helps to disguise this trend.

Alexandra Farquharson (14)
Sutton High School, Sutton

GREY PRISON

Kate looked into his startling blue eyes. Although he wasn't smiling, his eyes danced and twinkled merrily in the firelight. Neither of them spoke or even moved. Kate wasn't sure how it had all come to this. Her husband had left her, but it wasn't his fault. He thought it was patriotic. Fooled, like the rest of them. A small, sad, pitying smile spread across her face. He watched her gently, bemused. Kate reached out and touched the silver cross resting on his broad, scarred chest. Her smile faded as she remembered who she was in love with. Her mind flashed back to that cold, misty day out in the snow. The winter sun shone feebly through the grey clouds. Its soft shafts of light fell on the lonesome figure lying in the snow, blood flowing from a gunshot wound. She thought he was . . . but her hope faded almost as soon as it had come.

'Kate?' his soft, deep voice broke her train of thoughts. She blinked and managed another smile. She brushed his fringe out of his eyes. It was all over now. Patrick had gone to a better place and she was not alone.

God has a funny sense of humour she thought. Of all the people she could love . . . it just had to be him.

If only the world could stop fighting this war. They had seen the disaster of the first war, why did Britain join in a second time? If she could understand, so could the world. After all the man she was deeply in love with was a German . . .

Se-Yi Hong (14)
Sutton High School, Sutton

AFTERWARDS

Grey. That's all there is. That's what we did to this world. Anything that was once there is now gone. The dust is rising. It is like blanket over the ground. Even the sea is gone. Dust falls from the sky. There is no rain. The sun is blood-red. Darkness falls early. No one ventures out.

Deathly silence.

Look at what we had. Look at what we have done. The grass is always greener on the other side. That's what we were told. They who knew all. But there is no grass. I've been there. The bleak horizon lasts forever. There is no hope left in this fallen sky. Why? It was us. With our selfish hearts. No one thought - they only acted. I wish we'd thought. How I wish we had.

They all said it would save us. But it just killed us. There is no such thing as death anymore. We are dead. Dead to the world.

Helen Sumping (13)
Sutton High School, Sutton

LIVING LIFE IN FEAR

Daddy's home, I hope he's had a good day or Mummy will suffer. Sometimes I get in the way, but he pushes me harshly aside, I regain myself and run to my room. As I look through the keyhole I see Mummy on the floor crying, the evil outside is too much for my eyes. I look down wondering how long I will have to live like this. I start to weep, but I mustn't or Mummy will suffer even more and it'll be my entire fault.

The screams are too much for my ears, the cries for help. Dad abandons us and heads down the pub. I remove myself from my room and comfort Mummy like drink comforts Daddy. She doesn't want me to see her with black eyes. She's clutching her ribs, obviously in pain.

Mummy stands up for him like he's done nothing wrong, but I know different, I know I will always live my life in fear from a man that calls himself my father.

As Daddy returns home I run to my room. He mustn't find me with her. His footsteps become louder as he storms up the stairs, he calls after Mummy. His voice echoes in the hallway. I try to block out the noise; anger is filling up inside me, I ask myself why? The lock of my door turns; he's locked me in so I can't get in the way. I peer through the keyhole to see Mummy clutching the wall. I run to the door, I've got to help her.

Keri Farrow (13)
Sutton High School, Sutton

THRILLER KILLER

I open my eyes; my head is pounding from yesterday's kill. I lick the remaining blood off my lips and shower down the rest from my thick coat. Fresh, I go to find my next victim. Prowling the streets, lurking in the shadows. I mustn't be seen. 'What's this?' I see her heading for the woods. I scan her, watching. My heart stops, but the adrenaline pumps faster than ever. She's alone. My eyes light up yellow with a tint of fiery red as they always do on the 'hunt'. Slyly, I let her enter the woods, I'll follow her and when the time is right I'll strike.

Crossing the manic road, great stampedes of vehicles rush past me. I need to get across. She'll get away. *Beeeeeeep!* A great car is speeding towards me. With immense fear and anguish I lunge out of the way, diving onto the cold, hard pavement. She got away. My stomach is rumbling. I clutch it and sniff the air. Nothing.

I carry on searching for the next victim. This time I see a young, small boy. These are good because they can't escape. I bend my agile legs and leap over the dangerous river that is the road. He sees me coming and clumsily tries to scarper, but I'm too quick and take a great bite out of him. He screams an ear-piercing scream. I stroke his whiskers against mine and pick him up ready to take home to my family. *Rabbit, our favourite dish.* I am the killer.

Halima Koroma (12)
Sutton High School, Sutton

TO BE ALONE

It was grey and murky outside. I opened the door. A gust of icy wind greeted me, chilling my body. The ground was wet. I stepped onto it gingerly. Suddenly, I began to run. I ran slowly as if my muscles had been dormant for a long time. I accelerated and in about five minutes I reached the place of terror. I thought, because I was early, they might not be there. But they were. Like starving animals they pounced as I walked through the gate. They hurled insults at me. I braced myself as the insults died. I knew what was coming, I'd been through it time after time. They closed in on me like a pack of hyenas. I shut my eyes, curled my shoulders in to protect myself and covered my face with my hands. The punches and kicks began. My battered and bruised body screamed inside, but I remained silent. The attack would be harder if I screamed.

Soon they went. I heard the distant bell ring. I ran into the classroom. I realised as I felt the caked blood crack on my body that I hadn't cleaned myself up. My friends and tutor stared at me incredulously.
'What's happened?' my tutor asked.

I screamed, a high-pitched, piercing scream. A hollow silence remained as it died away. Then I turned and ran at full pelt. I had a vague idea of where I was going. I was going to be alone. Forever.

Katie Cattell (13)
Sutton High School, Sutton

LIFE AS AN ORPHAN

I am alone. No one is left to love me. No one to help me live my life. The life that I try to live is full of grey and black and, maybe if I am lucky, a splash of brown. People say that life can be filled with colours of buttercup-yellow, cherry-red and sky-blue. That's my dream, that I suppose will just never come true.

If I'm lucky a sparkle of glitter or a tiny ray of light may come into my life bringing a small chance of hope and happiness. As soon as it comes near and I am on the verge of receiving it, a whirl of evil black will come and whip it away.

I look at other children who have parents and a happy family. I am jealous of them, green with envy, not just because they have parents but also because they share love.

Love is a powerful thing as it comes from deep down inside you. It shows your true feelings. Love is the golden key to life. It unlocks your secrets and surprises. It is like the last thing that makes a volcano erupt. The splashes of hot, fiery, red lava are the unexpected surprises of joy that give you a 'hot', skip and jump in your life. People don't understand how much they should treasure love. They don't realise that this is what keeps them alive.

I can love, but I can never be loved in return.

Nadia Abdulla (13)
Sutton High School, Sutton

A Letter From A Soldier To His Love

My darling love,
I lay on my back every night staring at the stars and thinking of you and how our life would be if I hadn't have left for military service. Every day I go through the torment of not seeing you, but hundreds of lifeless bodies upon the ground, their lives stolen before my eyes and the tears burn. Never have I felt so much anger, but still the fear is creeping up on me like a monster in a dark alley.

Yesterday I saw my brother die from mustard gas. The sight of it tore me up inside: the blood and the pain. Another down. Will it be me next? *No!* I will survive this war for as long as I can, just so I can see your face and feel your sweet embrace.

I killed a few soldiers today; they fell to the ground. I felt revenge but a little voice inside was telling me to stop, but I can't. I passed a small village; bodies of children and parents lay pale and motionless upon the mud with tears in their bloody eyes and froth emerging from their mouths.

Black smoke appeared in the air where we made camp so we ran, as fast as we could. Some did not make it. One man looked at me with distinct desperate eyes calling for help. I now have the guilt of not going back hanging over me and it feels unbearable, but at least my heart is still pumping for the love of you.

Amal Khoury (13)
Sutton High School, Sutton

THE PRISON

Darkness envelops me, a world of nothing. I strike out wildly, my body thrashing from side to side, but I will never be able to penetrate the walls of my prison. Depression sets in. I can hear voices surrounding me, but I can never reach them. I'm slowly drowning in a pool of darkness as I desperately try to reach the surface. I cry out in the hope that someone can hear me, louder and louder until my lungs almost burst. I hear anxious replies, but they seem to float over me, coming from nowhere and heading for nowhere.

I feel like I'm nobody, shut off from the world. I lead a separate life, lonely and empty. A half-life, void of pure enjoyment, void of everything that I long for. I long for sunlight, for the colours of spring. I long to be free from this prison of darkness, to emerge blinking into glorious, golden sunlight. To experience everything that I hold dear.

Days run into night and night runs into day. Everything just feels the same to me now. I live on my positive thoughts; they are all I have left. The hope that I will be able to see again, to shake off blindness as if it is water.

Sarah Willis (13)
Sutton High School, Sutton

THE MINOTAUR

In the dark, mystical, shadowy world down under, there lives a creature, a dark, bitter thing that lives happily on human flesh. Many have attempted to kill the beast, but have failed and never been seen again.

The year 2003 has approached and the twelve who were chosen to try and rid everyone from the Minotaur have set sail and are to arrive right about now.

The cave in which the Minotaur lived wasn't as cold and damp as the twelve had anticipated, although it was as desolate as they had predicted. It was silent everywhere and you could hear the echoes of someone speaking.

Jessica, Spike, Michael, James, Mary, Alex, Robert, Andrea and Harriett had already tried, but there was no sign at all of them. Orlando now knew it was up to him to kill the Minotaur and pushed himself in even though he was terrified. He wasn't like the others though, he was clever and left a trail of string thinking that if he was going to leave the cave, the string would be the only thing to help him. Orlando had brown curly hair, was quite tall and most people were attracted to him.

Orlando was making his way slowly through the cave when he suddenly heard a roar from the beast and then was face to face with it. He then found himself rolling under and over the Minotaur, found a sharp stone and stabbed the Minotaur. He found his way out of the cave and gave a sigh of relief.

Jeyhan Mustafa (12)
Sutton High School, Sutton

A Day In The Life Of A Girl In Iraq

Bang! Yet again I wake up to an explosion. It deafens me. I pull off my blanket and go to check on my baby sister, she's crying. I try to soothe her back to sleep, but the screams of the people around our home keep her awake. A tear slips down my cheek. I feel so alone.

I place the child on my shoulder and keep rubbing her back, she's still sobbing, more faintly though. I think she can sense that her mother and father are dead, even if she is less than a year old. She's so small, she shouldn't have to go through this pain. I don't think it's fair.

But as Mama used to tell me, life isn't fair, it's not justice or peace, it's just life and you have to keep living it till it's your time. She was right; life isn't something you can just sit back and watch, it's something you work for, something to believe in.

I hear the bombs coming down outside and huddle in the corner with my now sleeping sister, she looks peaceful, happy. I cower down and pray that she will live, I don't mind if I die, but she's too young. Come to think of it, she's the only thing I have to live for anyway, she's everything to me. More than any possession.

I hear my death coming towards me and my life flashes before my eyes. All my memories, hopes, fears, dreams, opinions and beliefs crash down on me as the bomb does.

We both awoke to an explosion; we both fall asleep to one.

Eloise Kohler (12)
Sutton High School, Sutton

HOPE

It happened again, I don't know why she does it. She said it's all my fault that he left. I don't know why she hits me; I didn't mean to make her mad. I try to be a good girl for Mummy. I told her that she's not alone, I tried to tell her that I miss him too. She says mean things but it isn't her fault, she only hurts me when I am bad.

Sometimes when it's late and Mum's out I sit by the window and watch the passers-by. They don't know me; they can't feel my pain. I can. It screams inside me, why can't other people hear it too? They wouldn't care even if they could. I know they have their own pain, everyone does, but I just want someone to show that they care.

I miss it when Mummy leaves, but it's worse when she gets back. She acts like a crazy person, throwing things, using bad language. Once she nearly put a broken bottle through my face, I thought that I was going to die. I thought that my own mother was going to kill me. I cried myself to sleep that night. The new bruises hurt more than ever, but they will go even if worse scars will replace them. But the real scars are the ones that no one can see. I know it will be soon, she will hurt me again. Some people get love and hugs, I get abuse and pain. This world is not fair, my life is not fair. I just wish the pain would end.

Charlotte Knight (13)
Sutton High School, Sutton

TRAPPED

Dear Diary . . .

My life is in torment, but it won't be soon. My life is going to end and I'm glad. I'm sick of the pain, hurt and fear.

Who caused it? My mum's boyfriend. She doesn't know. Never will. I will leave her a note, telling her it wasn't her, but I won't tell her why. Never. But he will know. He will know why I'm gone. Why I'll never talk, see, hear, smell or feel again. That will be our secret. Forever.

My friends don't know. Never will. I envy them with their perfect lives. That's why I need to leave. Go to another place. A place where I will never feel pain, until the last second of my life. The last second of my life, it sounds so harmless, doesn't it? But when it comes down to it the last second of your life is everything, all your hopes, dreams, wishes and memories are lost forever. Well, it's lucky for me they've already gone. What am I saying? I've never had them, since he came five years ago.

This is my last night. Then I'll be gone. Forever. I have a disease, which is eating me from the inside. I can't win. Never will. This is the only way.

I don't feel anything. Should I? My mind is blank. I can't think. All I see is torture, pain and death around me. I feel trapped. So I need to escape. I'm going now. Goodbye, I'm *dea-*.

Rachel Johnston (13)
Sutton High School, Sutton

A Day In The Life Of A Spider

I'm not doing any harm as I sit in a corner watching the humans play. But a human will always come to shoo me away. As I wander into the kitchen I see the humans turn around and scream at the sight of me. I don't see how I can be so terrifying. I'm quite proud of my eight black legs that like to creep noiselessly across the wooden floor.

My favourite hobby is making webs by weaving in and out the silky thread. My web is also my food trap. I sit and wait; I see my food get entangled inside the silky thread. I like it when the raindrops fall from my web making it look like crystals, but the humans hate it and destroy my many hours of work.

I like escaping into the warmth of people's houses, but I have to be careful, so I walk in the shadows, trying to avoid the human's glare. My friends and I like scurrying from one place to another like it's a game trying to hide from the humans, but not all of us are successful.

Splat!

Rosanne Erman (13)
Sutton High School, Sutton

A Day In The Life Of A Blade

I lie there motionless. Soon she will be back from school. She will pick me up and shove me into her skin. All the blood will pour out of her wrist and I will be covered until the next morning when she will wash me under the ice-cold water.

I do not understand why she does it. I think it is because her mum hits her or she is bullied at school. If I could run away I would. I would go somewhere far away where she could not reach me. Where no one could reach me!

I do not like hurting her. I do not want to hurt anyone. I cry for her to stop, but I don't think she can hear me. It hurts me a lot more than it hurts her. Oh no, here she comes again. *No, please no.* She's done it again.

I lie here motionless, covered in blood. I cannot sleep with the red everywhere. I have a funny feeling about today. She lies there motionless. The bed sheets are wet from her tears of misery. Today she seems more peaceful while she sleeps. No, it cannot be, she's not moving at all. She's sleeping with a smile on her face. She's gone, she's really gone. *Wake up, please just wake up.*

We lie here motionless. I now know she's gone to a better place. She is happy and I will be happy when I get cleaned. *Thank you.*

Malini Desai (12)
Sutton High School, Sutton

SIR SPENCER AND THE BETRAYAL

It was dark. Sir Hector's blood stained the grass a deep crimson colour. Above his mangled body stood a menacing person. Piercing eyes shone, ears prickling, listening to the sounds in the wood, owls hooting, a snake eyeing up a mouse, waiting for the time when it would be no more. The man's head turned as some knights trampled through the undergrowth towards the victim and himself.

'What happened?' a knight in grey armour approached the men. 'My god, Sir Hector, dead! How did such a thing occur?'
'I am Sir Spencer. Hector knighted me just before the evil knight Sir Gringamour murdered him. I was powerless - a knife to my throat.' The man broke down into intense sobs.

The knight took Sir Spencer away to Camelot where he was welcomed as a brother by all. Before long, a man in red stood up. This had a colossal effect on everyone in the dinner hall; they all fell silent immediately.
'Sir Hector was a good knight. I'll therefore ride out and kill this man, Sir Gringamour.'

Arthur and Spencer rode off with Sir Lancelot unknowingly following behind them. He did not trust Spencer and wanted to keep a close eye on things. Sure enough, as the king and Spencer reached Gringamour's castle, a dozen knights ambushed them. Spencer sneered maliciously. A trap! Spencer was working for Gringamour! Spencer had murdered Hector! Spencer had betrayed the king! Lancelot stared open-mouthed at the struggling Arthur and the smirking Spencer, wondering what he could do.

Georgina Crate (12)
Sutton High School, Sutton

SATISFACTION

Have you ever wondered what it would be like to be someone else? To have their thoughts, feelings, emotions, hopes and fears. To experience what they'd do, meeting the people they'd meet, feeling their impressions and thoughts.

Who would you be? Someone who's rich or famous? Why? Do you think you would have more stability in your life and be free of worry? There would be no need to work hard, pass exams or interviews or gain a good job. There would be no need to worry whether you have enough money to pay for possessions or where your next meal comes from. You might want to be a celebrity perhaps? Be like a beautiful, glowing god or goddess, always the centre of attention and idolised. To have your talents recognised and use them to make your way in life.

Could you ever wish to be someone who is completely benevolent inside? Almost every person wants things; money, power, a bigger house or better looks than others. If you and a friend were competing for something and they won, could you ever feel completely happy for them without feeling a slight pang of jealousy?

If you could be someone else, would you find it easier to want to be someone who has a life of ease, an attractive or successful person? We find it easier to find faults with our appearance than with our characters.

If you could be anyone, would you choose to be yourself? Perhaps until we can learn to love ourselves inside and out, we can never be fully satisfied.

Katie Bolton (13)
Sutton High School, Sutton

THE SELFISH BOY

In a world a time ago there remained an island, an island of hope, of happiness and of love. This island was one that remained that of a secret, it was invisible to the naked eye. This island was inhabited by a race of people who contain only good and believe in only good and that evil has no place in their world.

Money has no place in this world as it is believed that money leads to greed and greed is that work of the Devil, an evil specimen in their world.

Such a perfect world is made up of perfect people, who become couples, who become families, who mix with other families to form new families. None of the same origin. Some old couples who have loved each other since first sight and others who came into the world as babies and others, young teenagers just starting out in this new world.

This is the tale of a boy swallowing up every last word that the Devil said. Jason was a selfish boy who had always received everything he asked for. He was very spoiled and he never returned any good deeds that people paid to him.

Many people warned him that he was defying the ways of his Lord and that it would all come to a sudden, unwieldy end. Jason led this unbelievably fantastic world to be destroyed by his evil ways and the work of the Lord in this special land was gone forever.

Franky Gaiger (13)
Sutton High School, Sutton

THE FATEFUL END

I was falling faster, faster by the second. My head became dizzy as I landed with a thump on the hard stone ground. My head was spinning so fast. The next thing I knew I'd woken up in a small room in what seemed to be a local bed and breakfast. I couldn't remember my actions the previous night. Someone must have rescued me and brought me here. I decided some fresh air would do some good.

I stepped out into the street, my long, fair hair blowing in the breeze. I had to find out where I was. The last thing I remembered was being out at the party with Taina and Kayleigh. We were walking home, but then I screamed and slipped and ended up here. I had to find Taina and Kayleigh. What had happened to them? Maybe they'd got hurt and been taken to the local hospital. Maybe they'd fallen out with me. My head started hurting thinking about last night's events.

I decided I'd go to the local hospital and see if they were there. It was my only way of finding them. I walked over to the reception area at Longdale hospital. The receptionist said that Taina and Kayleigh Brookes had been admitted to the hospital the previous night, but had died of brain damage in the early morning. What had happened that night at the party? Would I ever find out how Kayleigh and Taina had come to their fateful end?

Natasha Dubash (13)
Sutton High School, Sutton

THE WAR PRINCE

Chapter 1

In the dark days at the beginning of this kingdom, there came to pass an event which our whole history would be different without. It concerned the vigilance of one heroic young squire, often forgotten. He chose to take notice of a small shadow passing over the cliff top in front of him.

Christopher, son of the warlord Christian, being well trained in all matters of weaponry and such, soon brought the hawk above him tumbling to the ground, having shot quickly and accurately with his bow. When he crouched beside the bird to analyse his catch, he noticed a streak of blue amongst the dull red blood. Any other weak-hearted man would have been stricken with terror as this was the sure sight that the dreaded army of Vortimus was at hand. Christopher, being the true son of a lord, had a brave heart and hence did not take flight. Instead, he drew his sword and braced himself for battle. Throwing himself down on the edge of the cliff, the boy peered over, ready for whatever sight was to meet his eyes. Luckily it was far from the destruction he had imagined. His father's castle had stood firm against the army's attack, but the inhabitants now had no way of escape. They were enclosed by blue tents with banners picturing fierce hawks.

It was a siege. Christopher made his decision. He would not rush down and fight in vain. He now had a quest - to save his people.

Jennifer Crowhurst (13)
Sutton High School, Sutton

A Day In The Life Of A Soldier In The Iraq War

I have awoken from a dream where I envisioned my life as it should be. My family and I reunited, eating dinner, playing football - all the things I took for granted. My dream crashes to an end when I soon awake to the harsh realities of war in Iraq.

Every day I look around seeing the most courageous men this world has ever borne, but I simultaneously see one of the biggest mistakes mankind has ever inflicted upon this Earth - war!

Today is yet another day in this reconstruction of Hell. Commands are ordered as men are instructed to join the front line of the ground force. I step forward, obeying every word spoken. An expression of bravery spreads across my face, which gives a different picture from how I truly feel. The uncertainty of my fate haunts my soul.

We take our places, ready to destroy. First the feeling of trepidation fills my heart. Then feelings of bewilderment creep around, questioning the point of this mission. Thinking of the after-effects of this war fills my mind with indignation.

Daily this war takes its course, whilst stealing the lives of its innocent victims. The once courageous soldiers have changed to fearful, maimed men.

At night, fighting ceases. Thinking of tomorrow frightens me. I pray profusely to God telling him how thankful I am to be alive. Then comes the greatest emotion of all. The pride of fighting for one's country is immense.

Dulce et Decorum est. Pro patria mori.

Melanie Ranaweera (14)
Sutton High School, Sutton

THESEUS VS MINOTAUR

My name is Theseus, I'm King Aegeus' son and I killed the Minotaur! Every year, 14 people were taken to feed this monster and I decided to stop it.

Dad kept begging me to reconsider and as I was nervous I almost agreed, but I didn't. So Dad told me to change the boat's sails from black to white if I'd killed it.

We soon arrived in Crete. King Minos' beautiful daughter, Ariadne, saw me - we got talking and fell in love! When I told her what I was going to do she gave me some thread and a sword. 'Unwind the thread as you go, you can find your way out by following it,' she explained.

So I apprehensively entered the maze, leaving a thread trail.

I walked until I was exhausted. Suddenly I saw the monster and as it attacked me I plunged my sword into it. It gave one last bellow, then died. I jumped around celebrating before following the thread out.

I met Ariadne and we sailed to Naxos Island where I dreamt that she would live happily with Dionysis. I unhappily left her and sailed for home. Unfortunately, I forgot to change the sails so my dad feared the worst, jumped into the sea and drowned.

By the time I reached the shore I had mixed feelings - I was King of Athens, but my dad was dead. In my grief I declared that I would be a good ruler like my dad.

Kathy Stevens (13)
Sutton High School, Sutton

MORE LEAVE THE PLANET

The Informative
22 July 2075

Yesterday NASA sent another family to live on Mars. They will join five families who have been living there for between 8-9 months. This latest family to agree to NASAs space plan are the Thomsons. They went through intense training to be able to adapt to their new home. They will be living in a five-bedroomed house in Armstrong, a newly constructed town that is said to be like Earth, but without the grass. The town has been constructed in a dome-like structure, allowing the inhabitants to have a sufficient amount of oxygen. There is also access to water as by controlling temperatures at the polar ice caps, scientists have managed to retrieve water.

The project has been successful and has been encouraged by governments around the world. They hope that by 2095 more than 500,000 people will be living on Mars as there has been a massive increase in population and a lack of global resources. Many fear that if the Earth is not evacuated soon, the human race will become extinct in a massive flood as the poles are rapidly melting because of global warming.

It seems that the Thomsons will be followed by many other people in the future. The Thomsons are said to feel privileged to take part in this experiment. Their youngest child said she would miss her friends and her dog, but was ecstatic about going to Mars. NASA plans to send another three families in two months time.

Jalpa Patel (13)
Sutton High School, Sutton

My Encounter With The Lady

I was a traveller. I never stayed in a place long enough to see the moon twice. Here, where I stand, I have seen countless moons. My eyes are still fixed on the spot where she stood, My mind wanders though my body cannot . . .

I remember ages and moons ago. I travelled. I aimed for Herculaneum, but was diverted by tales of a lady with killer looks. As I ran to find her, civilisation began to grow around me. A castle rose from behind a dune. Soon the sun set and it was night. It was not a cold night, but as I stared up at the bare stone walls, I shivered. I was scared, openly afraid. I knew that I had found her. There was no reason for me to keep away, no fence, but strangely I wished for one. I should have turned and ran, but instead I kept going.

The castle walls were bathed in moonlight. Our eyes met. I stopped running. In fact, I stopped moving, breathing. She stood there, not quite smiling. Her looks were terrifying, mesmerising. The snakes were laughing at me. She turned and walked away. I tried to follow her but my body would not obey me.

A long time has passed, but I still look the same. My fate is set in stone. I stand, trapped in the body of a young man.

Charmaine Yeoh (12)
Sutton High School, Sutton

A Day In The Life Of William Graves: A Soldier Living In The Trenches Of World War One

Dearest Eliza,

To start with I will mention how much I miss you, however, I know that I must stay to carry out my duty, for my country and the Lord above.

I cannot even begin to describe the trench warfare. It is horrifying and I wish for no one to see what I have seen in this war . . . or what my nose has smelt.

The day starts half an hour before sunrise, which is marked by a 'stand to' along the parapets. The men find it hard to disregard the stench so early in the day. It is a mixture of unburied corpses, compounded stagnant mud and stale sweat. After the sentries have been posted; we eat breakfast. Our meals are monotonous, we receive ration biscuits, hard as rock. In order to break them some men hit them with their bayonets. Then comes the bread and the 'bully beef'.

The day passes by with routine jobs, mostly to do with keeping the trenches in good repair; this includes the removing of the bones piercing through their shallow burials, and the elimination of the uncountable number of rats and lice that infest the trenches. I cannot stand them, the rats, for now I can hear the straw writhing with them in the night. These tedious tasks continue until a final 'stand to' at dusk.

I must end my letter here as sunrise is close approaching and there is a long day ahead of me.

With all my love
William Graves

Nabila Fazal (13)
Sutton High School, Sutton

A Day In The Life Of A Homeless Lady

She has absolutely nothing - no home, no friends, no love, nothing at all. She doesn't even have a name. Well, nobody knows it. She begs on the street hoping, wishing that someone would drop a single coin in her paper cup that she has used for many years, so many years that it is now rotting. This single coin might even be enough for her to treat herself to a cup of tea or coffee, which she might not have had for weeks. She is alone and cold inside, like a stranger to herself, but her heart is anything but cold. Nobody cares about her. She's quiet, trying not to bother passers-by, but inside she wants to scream. Nobody knows how she feels. Nobody is there for her, to take her hand or comfort her in a way she may be able to build her strength. Her face is raw dullness because nothing has made her smile in years. She may have never smiled in her life it's a mystery. Her homeless life in her only memory - a *bad* memory that lives with her still, not going but permanently staying there in her head. She feels left out of the world she was brought into, to be part of. People hate her. They think she's dirty and ugly and prefer not to take one step near her. They don't understand her. She's confusion, an illusion to them and to herself.

Yes, she has nothing, but does this mean she is nothing?

Eleanor Wright (13)
Sutton High School, Sutton

RELEASED

Another beautiful, clear day, but not for me. It's only another bruise. It's only another cut.

My parents glance at me with cold eyes as I sit, back bolt upright, in my chair. The kitchen is silent, except for the low buzz that comes from our broken fridge. No one has their elbows on the table. Everyone is staring into their food, stuffing it into their mouths.

As I bring the toast to my mouth, some crumbs spill on the floor. By the time I realised, it's too late. My mother noticed first. Her hands slap my cheek so hard that her hand is imprinted on it. She commands me to pick up every crumb and shouts at me for being so careless.

School is no better. I sit next to no one. I have no friends. I'm bullied with sticks, stones, sand and sometimes even fire.

It's a cookery lesson. After getting the chopping board, I pick up a knife. I gaze down at it, wondering how many times I have thought of cutting one of my arteries going through my wrist. But I decided this morning that dying painfully is not a good idea. I decided that being hit by a train wouldn't be so bad.

After school I walk on the tracks. The silver metal reflects back the sunlight and seems welcoming, like a real home. I see a train coming my way with tremendous speed. I close my eyes. May my soul rest in peace.

Ai Taniuchi (13)
Sutton High School, Sutton

A Day In The Life Of A Book

Many times in my existence I have been opened and closed to suit people's imagination.

My days are spent alone, squashed on the shelf between the world atlas and the big encyclopaedia. My victim returns. I dust myself off to seduce my prey. I have made him an addict to my lush brown paper pages and my bold black writing.

The night is young as he takes me from my secluded home and he collapses on the sofa. He opens me. My flesh is bared. My quest is clear. Start. I suck his imagination like a Hoover so he is completely consoled by me. I brainwash, like a wave across his mind, with my mood swings I change to his likeness in order to keep me in his ever happiness.

I can be serious, funny or even make you cry. I hold the answer to everything. I come as paperback or hardback. I come by the Internet or at shops or by mail.

I can capture your inner being and read between the lines to create a deeper being.

I enhance your imagination to dream of a different world. I scare you a fright and take hold your pleasant nature until all that is left is a soulless, mindless creature that relies on my demon-living pages and bright pictures.

So children, next time your parents and teachers say, 'You must read, books are pleasure,' remember what I have told you today, the secrets of my success.

Chukwunyere Samuel (12)
Sutton High School, Sutton

LIFE AS A VICTORIAN MOTHER

My name is Pollyanna Smith. I am wife to Tom and mother to three. At the moment my middle child, Sally, is very ill. Tom and I know she has typhoid as she has been drinking lots of the sewage water lately.

We're living in London. It's very crowded in our back-to-back home which we share with two other families! I wish we hadn't moved, but Tom said we had to move to London to find work. Work I say! Ever since we moved Sally's been ill and that baby keeps crying. It's doing my head in! I've tried everything for Sally from fresh fruit to those horrible pills they sell on the market - nothing seems to work. And Peter, it's no good for him either. He's only eight but he is already working in one of those noisy factories. It exhausts him. He tries his hardest and gets bread for me which is . . . helpful, but I do wonder where he gets it from as it can have pieces of dead animals in it.

There the baby goes again, better go and give it a drop of gin to tire it. Tom should be back from working on the railway tunnel soon.

When I'm looking after Sally I'm secretly hoping that I will not catch typhoid. I don't think Tom could cope. Sally will not survive another week. Forgive me.

Sarah Haville (12)
Sutton High School, Sutton

TIME TO TELL

Danni had known that it was different from the beginning, but not this dissimilar, not so unlike that they would drive her away. Since that day in the car when they had approached the area she knew things would be a lot different.

The houses were smaller and there were no ornamental cars. She knew that now Dad had left everything was going to adjust. Her new room was smaller than their old toilet and Grandma just made things inferior by exclaiming all would be fine and she would look after them as well as possible.

Then along came Hallie and Mel. They seemed friendly at first and listened with ardour to what she had to say about her old life in Knightsbridge. Everything seemed perfect, but it wasn't for Michelle. Michelle had lost her best friends to a girl who had all she'd ever wanted and was more popular than she was. So, she'd decided to do something about it.

Unexpectedly, Danni's possessions began to recede including her school books. When asked why she hadn't handed in her homework, Danni started telling teachers that they had been taken from her bag. Obviously, not believing her, they had told her off and soon Danni was in more trouble than she could imagine. Deeming Danni had become a rebel, Hallie and Mel went back to Michelle. Now, Danni was alone and in deep trouble.

The door creaked open and she stepped in. It was time to tell . . .

Natasha Ward (13)
Sutton High School, Sutton

THE LOCKED DOOR - MYTH

There is a room in a house, in a town, in a faraway country, that no one dares enter. The door has been locked for seventy-five years and in that time, no living soul has set foot inside.

Every night as the town clock strikes twelve, the most spine-chilling scream heralds the start of a ritual that turns the bravest of men into quivering jellyfish. Many have tried to spend the night alone in this house, but few have lived to tell of its secrets. Too often, come daybreak, their corpses are found, stiff with fear, by the window or the front door, through which they had been trying to escape.

So what is it abut this haunting that makes it so terrifying? Is it the heavy hobnail boots that pace up and down the wooden floorboards all night? Is it the constant wailing and chattering that float through the house and penetrate your sleep? Or, perhaps, it's the tiny trickle of blood that seeps through the ceiling and drips off the light bulb in the bedroom. Others say that the noise of the ghost hurling objects around the room would be enough to drive them mad.

The truth is that behind that locked door at the top of that house, in that town, in that far-away country, there are noises to terrify everyone. Except perhaps a child, a small innocent child, too young to understand what lies behind the noises that she is hearing.

Rebecca Rainback (13)
Sutton High School, Sutton

A Day In The Life Of An Evacuee

I am a parcel; labelled, addressed and packed off to the country. The ominous clouds overhead only deepen the forlorn emotions inside me. I am leaving home for the first time, bundled away to the safety of Wales, although this isn't what has whirled up the storm churning in my stomach and put out the light in my eyes. This worry and guilt is caused because I have abandoned Mother to the ravages of war.

Oh I tried to persuade her to let me stay! I would help her through; we could have lent on one another. She has weakened since the death of my father; indeed it was a punch in the stomach to us both. She tells me that Hitler has taken away her husband; he is not going to take away her daughter. My father would have replied, *'Don't be angry and sad that I am gone, just be happy that I was here.'*

My mind is terrorised, scarred with images of a damaged London. I am trying so hard to be brave but I am terrified that my new family won't like me. I have brought my 'trophy' collection along to show the other children. These are pieces from planes and bombs that us Londoners collect. I have a real whopper - an unexploded cartridge!

I was desperate to stay and now I long to return. After all, if I die I will be one in thousands; the country no longer mourns the death of one child.

Alice Kendle (12)
Sutton High School, Sutton

THE DARE

As the two trembling girls pushed open the creaky door, they gingerly stepped inside the old dusty house. The floorboards creaked under their weight. The girls looked at each other with their knees trembling and hearts pounding.

'I don't like this place, I'm so scared, we have to leave,' whispered Sarah.

'No, we can't, this is a dare, remember?' said Alice, even though she knew that she wanted to leave herself. 'If we leave now we'll be called wimps and we'll get teased tomorrow at school.'

'You're right,' replied Sarah, 'the dare was to stay in here for five minutes and that is what we are going to do.'

The two girls hugged each other tightly and crept forward a few more paces. Alice kept looking at her watch to see how long they had to go; they had only been in there for half a minute!

'What are you doing in my house?' said an eerie, whispery voice from upstairs.

The girls clutched each other so they could hardly breathe; Sarah had gone so white she was as pale as a ghost.

'Get out of my house!' screamed the voice.

The girls were almost in tears but they knew that they couldn't leave.

Suddenly, they heard an ear-piercing shriek from upstairs. The girls started to whimper, they were so afraid. Then they heard the terrifying voice again.

'Sarah . . . Alice . . . if you don't leave my house now you'll be next . . . '

Claire Caswell (12)
Sutton High School, Sutton

BULLY

He was wearing his ripped trousers, mud-stained shirt untucked and baseball cap, looking really threatening when he approached me . . . the school bully had decided to pick on me.

I'll tell you exactly what happened. It was at lunch, I was playing a game of football and accidentally stumbled into Luke. He took it the wrong way and demanded that I meet him after school at the gates. So, I did. He ordered me to hand over my phone and money or he'd beat me up!

I felt really stupid; there was nothing else I could do so I just handed over what he wanted.

I regret doing this, what was I thinking? How could I have let him get away with such an appalling thing?

I needed to tell someone - my mum. It was the only way to sort things. She went into school and complained the next day, which was extremely embarrassing for me. I could see the kids sniggering and whispering about her. Her clothes were so old-fashioned; I just wanted the ground to swallow me up.

But it was all worth it as Luke came up to me the minute my mum left and apologised! He gave all my belongings back.

The head teacher must have made him own up and give back my things which is quite humorous really. He is also in detention.

Luke must feel such a fool, and pretty humiliated!

I'm never going to let bullies bring me down again.

Emily Ure (13)
Sutton High School, Sutton

LAST DAY

Mary passed Donsil Brook on her tedious journey to the factory that morning. As Mary looked down upon the clumps of daffodils along the stream, she wondered to herself what life would be like if she didn't have to work in Mr Arkwright's beastly mill. She could have the freedom of her childhood and regain her strength.

As she hoisted up her filthy skirt, the factory bell sounded and she hastily made her way over the bridge. The mill at Cromford had always scared her, however the early spring sunshine somehow softened the harsh realities of the inside.

Mary could hear the machines violently rattling as she saw Arkwright solemnly stride past. She reached for a basket and made her way to the water frame where she worked.

The day passed and night was drawing in. She could see the sunset from her frame and she was almost finished. She felt faint and was exhausted from the weary day. Mary carefully crawled under the machine to reach the last piece of wool when she felt her hair being pulled. She started to shake and as she put her hands up to try and free herself, she felt a trickle of blood down her back. She experienced a sharp rush of pain, like a wound dipped into salt water. Her skirt had gone a deep red colour and she was unable to move. She had lost consciousness and was slowly drifting into a different world.

Helen McEwan (14)
Sutton High School, Sutton

BLUEBELL CHECKERS

The curtain blew backwards and forwards in time with the vigorous wind that was coming through the open window. Apart from the sound of this, the room was silent.

Suddenly there was a creak as if a door was opening - Nicky sat up bolt upright and looked around her - the door was closed. She studied the room carefully, then she spotted the doll's house. Down in the corner of the room there was a bright green door opening. It had a silver letter box and pink flowers painted in the shape of a heart - it was the doll's house door! Nicky stepped out of bed and peered into one of the windows.

Inside she could see the blue bathroom and the silver bath, sink and towel rail. There was another creaking sound, a small gasp and the door slammed back into place. Nicky poked her finger at the door, but she couldn't open it. It was as if someone had bolted it right to the top. But who? Nicky kept poking - eventually she opened it.

There was a split second of silence and then a girl stepped out of the house. Her ruby-red lips were pressed together and her blonde curls were tied into a tight bun. Her eyes were like bluebells, matching her checked pinafore and stripy blouse. Her feet were buckled fast with tiny black ballet shoes and her hands, which were fastened to her hips, were wrapped in black leather gloves.

'What do you want?'

Danielle Tanton (14)
Sutton High School, Sutton

WINTER 1953

I know *that* last time definitely was the last time; I knew this as I gazed at the blood trickling down the blunt knife in my hand. It had gone on too long; I mean seven times is a lot for a man of 34. But now as I had just committed my bloodiest and worst murder ever, the chase is probably coming to an end as the police have been on my tail since my third. Now you may *wonder* how I committed my final murder, so this is my account.

As the hour hand fell dead on nine, I stepped out of the red Volkswagen I'd found near Waterloo Station. I hadn't planned how I would do it, nor did I know my victim. But I knew that I was going to commit this murder and nothing would stop me. So, as my urge to kill hit me, I approached the door and rang the doorbell.

'Mini cab, Miss.'
'No, sorry, I didn't order a mini ca . . . '

I stuffed her mouth with a hankie and watched her eyes as they stared at the steel knife with fear. Then, I pulled at the rope surrounding her neck and held on for almost three seconds and let go. It was then that the knife came to use as I stabbed her chest with the cold blunt steel ten or twelve times, then I watched as she gradually slipped away and took her last painful breath.

Kate Martin (13)
Sutton High School, Sutton

THE ANCIENT MYTH OF EASTER ISLAND

Long ago there lived a giant named Laurel. He was a skilled sculptor but he was also poor and struggled to survive on stale crusts of bread. His one valuable possession was his beautiful daughter, Zella, who looked after him.

One day he was summoned before the king and asked to sculpt some majestic statues for his new palace. This was a great honour and Laurel was overjoyed. For one hundred days he slaved over the project and on the final day he brought Zella with him so she could see for herself the marvels he had created.

Upon seeing Zella, the king fell deeply in love and resolved to marry her. When he heard of this, Laurel was defiant.
'I forbid you to marry my daughter, for she is all I have! I would die of a broken heart if she left me!'
'You will die for this insult!' the king shouted angrily, drawing his royal sword.

Laurel flung his statues into a bag and fled from the palace, the king in hot pursuit. The chase continued for seven days and seven nights, until Laurel's woven sack split and the elaborate statues plunged to the ground!

The king laughed so much his anger cooled, and he returned to his palace and married Zella. Laurel settled on an island nearby, where he continued his sculpting until he died. The statues that fell from his bag can be seen today, on an island in the Pacific known as Easter Island.

Helen Thorpe (13)
Sutton High School, Sutton

A Day In The Life Of A Koala

I am a koala called Betty. I live in the Lone Pine Koala Sanctuary in Australia. My baby is six months old. He spends a lot of time in my pouch feeding on milk and sleeping. He is getting older and now climbs out of my pouch and onto my back.

In the morning I take a long time to wake up. As soon as I wake up I am hungry, so I start to eat eucalyptus leaves, which is my favourite food. Feeding makes me tired so I fall asleep again. I go to sleep sitting in the eucalyptus tree where the branches fork.

After another sleep I wake up and spend some time grooming my fur. It is very hot today and I spend the rest of the day dozing.

Some days the sanctuary is open to the public. People come and stare at us and take flash photographs, which is very annoying. The keeper who looks after us, Mark, allows the tourists to hold my baby and me. It is very strange being handled by someone different and I am always glad to get back to my eucalyptus tree.

At night, when it gets dark I climb down the tree and move to another one. When I am on the ground moving from tree to tree I must be careful, in case I get attacked by an animal such as a dingo. I climb up another tree to the top branches to feed on shoots and leaves.

Charlotte Howson (12)
Sutton High School, Sutton

A Day In The Life Of A Wedding Ring

As I sat in the shop window watching as all my friends were proudly placed into their posh boxes, I jumped to find a man staring at me and pointing. The glass window was opened and the shop manager carefully took me out.
The same man as before inspected me, he looked ecstatic and said, 'I'll take it!'
Wait, was it my time? Then the shop manager proudly lifted me into a navy blue and extremely posh box and closed the lid.

Inside it was comfy and I loved the soft silk and velvet that covered the inside. Then I felt myself being slipped into a pocket and being taken to a new destination.

I was resting in my box when it was opened and outside were very smartly dressed people and a beautiful room. I was enjoying this, I was placed on a velvet pillow and taken to the front of the room.

There was a ceremony going on, people were weeping and words were said. Then I was placed on the finger of a very beautiful lady, she was dressed in a white dress with a veil over her head. Then I realised that I was sitting below another ring, which had a gleaming crystal, although it was not as big as mine. I smiled and knew that I would love my new home.

Santina Philips (12)
Sutton High School, Sutton

UFO VIDEOTAPED IN TEXAS

Exclusive

Yesterday, on Saturday, October 20th, FOX News aired a startling video showing an oblong UFO in flight near the International Airport in Austin, Texas.

The sight was strange in the skies over Austin. No one knows just what it was, but it was enough to have the FBI rushing to take a look.

One of FOX's videographers was shooting a video of a plane taking off from the Austin International Airport. At the same time, a strange object streaked through the sky. The photographer tells us he did not notice the fast-moving object zooming across the sky until he played back the video in slow motion.

We are told the object did not show up on radar, but it was described as 'long, slender, with two sets of wings'.

A local resident, who witnessed the broadcast said, 'It was faster than any aircraft I have seen. It was so fast; it was only on screen for four frames. The local weather reporter said it was at an altitude of 4,000 feet, based on the type of cloud it flew through'.

The FOX TV station sent their tapes to the FBI and now an investigation is under way to determine exactly what the object is, whether it is an 'alien spacecraft' or just a military missile. The FAA has said that whatever the object is, it did not show up on local radar. The FBI will not comment while it is investigating.

Emy Calder (14)
Sutton High School, Sutton

A Day In The Life Of Aliysa Cammy

At lunchtime registration, Mr Blank (our *cool* form tutor) shouted down the register and when he came to the last couple of names, he paused and smiled, then he called out, 'Is there a Kyle Marsh here?' There was no reply so he called out again, 'Is Kyle Marsh here?'

Suddenly someone burst in through the doors, he was the fittest guy I had ever seen. He was tall, dark and handsome and he had the bluest eyes I had ever seen.

He walked up to Mr Blank and apologised, he said he had got lost because he was new. Mr Blank reluctantly accepted his apology and told Kyle to sit in a free space, which was right next to me - not because I was a Larry but because my partner was away! As he sat down next to me he said rather cheekily, 'Hi my name is Kyle, I'm new around here, can you guide me around?' and gave me a heart-melting smile.
I felt myself blushing but I managed to say, 'My name is Aliysa Cammy, sure I'd love to!'

Then we talked and exchanged mobile numbers (I could see there was chemistry between us). I looked over my shoulder and could see my two best friends green with envy and I felt invincible.

Kyle and I had a lot in common, like he was good at sports and I was the female captain of all sports in our school. There was also a male. This made me think this could end up with us being more than just friends.

Christina Kang (14)
Sutton High School, Sutton

THE CHIMNEY BOY

Arriving at number 56 is a splendid sight. The house is perfect, any young boy's dream; to be looked after by the maids; to have endless amounts of toys and all the food you could possibly want.

I walked up the steps to find the milk still at the front doorstep, old Maggie can't be up or the milkman was early.

Entering the house I saw the housekeeper, she is a scary lady so I try to avoid her. She has her morning chat with the owner whilst I sneak past. I always seem to get lost in this house and finding one of the many fireplaces is challenging.

The first I go to is the one in the dining room which has huge slabs of marble around it. Getting into the chimney is easy as I am quite small but getting up it is harder. My broom is quite heavy but I am able to get it up and out the top of the chimney. I can feel the dust falling on my face and it's difficult to brush off. I try to blow it away with my mouth but it has decided to stay put. As I touch the wall of the chimney I feel heat rising.

Somebody's coming, I can hear their footsteps on the wooden floor. They've forgotten that I'm here and lit a fire. My feet are starting to get nearer to the flames. If I fall then I'll burn. What am I going to do?

Emma Robertson (14)
Sutton High School, Sutton

FORGOTTEN

It must have been late morning when I came back into the world. As I awoke, I could hear faint whispers nearby. I slowly opened my eyes to see a young girl sitting beside me, smiling with huge, excited, blue eyes. She had a gorgeous face, but I did not recognise it. She dropped my hand, which she had been firmly clutching for the past few hours and ran away, into the blur.

I slowly began to realise that I was in a hospital, surrounded by plain white walls with monitors attached to almost every part of my body.

A man, woman and the same girl came towards me. The woman looked into my eyes and smiled with relief, hugging me, unwilling to let go. When she looked at me again, I could see she had tears flowing down her pale face. 'Sarah? It's me, your mum! Sarah?' By this time her face showed a worried expression.
'Who are you?' I asked.
'Sarah? Don't you remember? You have been in a coma for the last three years. You had that accident . . . in the car.'
Trying to smile, she could hardly talk, her tears were choking her. I looked at her with disbelief. I asked her questions I needed answers to.
'Who is Sarah? Who am I?'
She threw her head into my lap, crying terribly. I could feel pain again, my eyes went blurry and I slipped back into unconsciousness.

I never saw my mother's face again.

Lauren Healy (13)
Sutton High School, Sutton

GREY NOVEMBER

We formed an orderly queue outside the formidable building. Here and there a baby wailed and was hushed by its distracted mother.

I gazed blearily up at the grey, menacing building with its cracked windowpanes. A slate hung off the wall but it swung so tempestuously in the wind and rain that it was unreadable. Smog escaped the enormous, blackened chimneys, enveloping the rooftops of Victorian London. *A right pea-souper* Dad would have called it; but now he was too drunk to be aware of his miserable surroundings.

Mother looked around despondently at her malnourished children. Their pale, emaciated faces gazed blankly ahead. Her husband's eyes rolled in his head and he leaned unstably on his eldest son.
'You there!' The large, savage finger of the proprietor, Mr Blacklock, pointed at my broken mother. She stepped obediently forward.
'You can take that girl,' he indicated towards me, 'and help with the weaving.'

My mother clasped my hand tightly and we entered the building. As we walked along the narrow passage, we heard Mr Blacklock instructing my brothers to help break stones for a new road.
'I'm afraid we have no room for drunken wretches. You can take yourself off,' Mr Blacklock informed my father.

I looked up to see my mother's face. A single tear streamed down her weather-beaten face, but she showed no other remorse. It splashed to the flag-stoned floor and we never spoke of my father again.

Emma Rice (14)
Sutton High School, Sutton

COMPLICATED

'How could you do this to me?' Her hateful voice hit me in the face as if I'd been slapped. Her eyes were dark and the tears falling down her cheek didn't make me feel any better.
'I'm sorry,' I replied meekly for the umpteenth time. I had honestly lost count of the times I had said that word and I was starting to hate it. 'I told you I never meant for it to happen.' I looked away, but not before seeing the hurt in her eyes. She was my best friend, or had been.
'I still don't understand *how* you could do it,' she said quietly.
As if I didn't feel bad enough. 'Me neither,' was the only reply I could come up with. She must hate me so much. I hated myself.
'Can I just ask you one question?' The directness of her voice startled me. I nodded.
'Did you only do it because you thought I wouldn't be there at the party or just because you were jealous?'
'Neither,' I replied. More lies. Would it be so hard to tell her that I had been jealous of her and her boyfriend ever since they met? Yes.

She looked at me. I looked at her. Our eyes locked. She had given me a chance to explain everything and I had just let it go.

She turned around and walked away, not looking back once and I knew that nothing would ever be the same again.

Seville Haghbedeh (14)
Sutton High School, Sutton

HUNTING A MASTERMIND

I tried to block the memories out of my head, so I decided to go to work and distract myself. I still had those horrific visions that were hovering in my thoughts, but I had to be ready to solve the case that killed so many.

The clock struck twelve as I arrived at the scene of the crime. I showed my badge before I entered the doomed house of *Lizze Crenshaw*. I wandered around for a few moments, but then decided to see the crime scene.

I walked upstairs and the door creaked open. There she was. Her body hadn't been taken away; her neck was hanging from a rope attached to the ceiling. Blood had made a large puddle on the floor under her body; the room fell silent as the other detectives stood amazed at the sight. I was in a state of shock. My body quivered at the sight of her and now I had goosebumps.

After gazing at the sight I started to make evidence. I took a picture of her body and then I looked around the room for any hidden clues. I searched for an hour and found a piece of old cloth cut out into the shape of *'A'*. I didn't take that much notice but decided to take a photograph for evidence.

As I walked out of the house I realised that I was hunting for a mastermind and this case was going to be a challenge for my mind.

Skeena Hamdani (14)
Sutton High School, Sutton

A Day In The Life Of My Dog

I was woken this morning by Nancy opening the kitchen door. I was so excited to see her that I jumped up at her. I laddered her tights and she got angry and shut me out in the garden. But she soon forgot and when she let me in she had made my breakfast. I devoured it hungrily and pushed open the back door.

I was playing on the wet, dewy grass when I heard a voice shout, 'Bazil, come in!'
I ran inside to find that the rest of the family were now in the kitchen. I said hello to everyone, being careful not to rip anymore tights. I settled down on my bed. Then Nancy called, 'Bazil, come on boy!' that's my favourite part of the day. A ten minute walk to the bus stop with Nancy and her dad and her dad walks me back again.

I played and slept for most of the day. Then Nancy's mum called, 'Bazil, Bazil, time to get Nancy.' I ran to the front door where Nancy's mum was waiting. She fastened my lead onto my collar and we set off to the bust stop.

I was so excited and I was running around and Nancy's mum got quite impatient. When she got off the bus I ran up to her and rubbed my head against her legs.

An amazing typical day for a small Scottie dog!

Nancy Godden (11)
Sutton High School, Sutton

DARK SIGHT

I walked calmly down the street, looking up at the stars twinkling like frosty diamonds in the sky. I never expected what came next.

The clammy hand reached around my mouth, taking me completely by surprise. That hand . . . it still sends shivers down my spine. It was so weathered and icy - as if it had been buried in a graveyard. He covered my eyes as well; as if this had all been rehearsed before in some nightmare far away. I heard a grating noise and then I was going down, down into the depths.

It was the smell that struck me first. It made me swoon and I felt my hand slip from the rail it was clinging to. The man held me tightly as we descended the never-ending slope into the sewers.

'We'll stop here for the night,' he muttered to himself like a madman, 'and then we'll go to *them.*' He said the last word with such terror, that I myself started to shiver with apprehension. Then it hit me. I was going to die. I lay down in the squalor of the sewer, lulling myself to sleep.

The dark closed all around me, smothering all of my hope with fear. The dark was mocking me - taunting from the safety of its den. I don't remember what came over me, but I plunged into the water.

This wasn't the life I wanted to lead when I escaped that night. I'm still lost in the sewer and eat rotten food from the sewer. My old life is over.

Catherine Kilkenny (12)
Sutton High School, Sutton

A Modern Day Story Of Vertumnus And Pomona

The Taylors were an unusual family. Rachel was of this class and no one excelled her in love of the garden and the culture of fruit. She cared not for forests and rivers, but loved the cultivated country and trees that bear delicious apples. Her right hand bore its weapon, not a chocolate bar but a pruning knife. Armed with this, she busied herself at one time to repress the too luxuriant growths; and curtail the branches that straggled out of place; at another, to split the twig and insert therein a graft, making the branch adopt a nurseling not its own. She took care too, that her favourites should not suffer from drought and led streams of water by them, that the thirsty roots might drink.

This occupation was her pursuit, her passion; and she was free from that which Venus inspires. She was not without fear of the country people and kept her orchard locked and allowed no men to enter.

The boys and men would have given all they possessed to win her and so would old Simon, who looks young for his years and Peter, who wears a garland of pine leaves around his head. But Oliver loved her best of all; yet he fared no better than the rest. Oh how often, in the disguise of a butcher, did he bring her meat in a basket. With a hay band tied round him, one would think he had just come from turning over the grass. Now he bore a pruning hook and impersonated a vine-dresser, all for her. The things people do for love!

Anna Russell (12)
Sutton High School, Sutton

An Extract Of Lucy's Diary

High-spirited we pile outside. Despite the rain, we chat and giggle, awaiting the arrival of parents. The thought gradually dawned on me as I remember tonight I will not be enjoying their company. I will be at home, lonely, sad and bored, whilst my friends - they will be having fun - exciting, girlie fun, all the fun you want to be having after an event like that.

The car pulls up - 1, 2, 3 and 4, slam the doors shut and as I wave goodbye, how I long to be within those doors, having the fun a girl my age should. It's OK, Lizzie's still waiting, aren't you? Wait, why are you leaving? *Slam.* All gone, now I am completely alone.

It's strange how the rain feels so much colder on your own. The wind bites through you much harder when you aren't chatting. I stand motionless, staring out into the rain, still longing to be with my friends.

15 minutes go by. After that, each minutes seems more like an hour and the rain is still falling, the wind still biting, but now loneliness is also eating me.

After what seems so long, after everyone else has left, after the cold has got right to my bones, my car pulls up. Arms crossed I walk to it and climb in, pathetically. I sit hunched in the corner - head against the window, staring, not saying a word.

Sophie Horgan (12)
Sutton High School, Sutton

THE RING

I, Margo Brantley aged eleven, was playing ball with my dog, Shadow, when the ball suddenly rolled into the distant bushes in my garden in East Sussex. I scrambled to get it, but something was in the way - a golden ring! I gracefully put it on, but immediately, it took me inside a multicoloured tube. It went black.

I opened my eyes - it was extremely bright and cloudy. There were people flying around with wings, then I read a sign, it said *Heaven*. I couldn't believe my eyes as an angel flew by.
She stopped and said, 'Fly, fly away and away, into the depths of a black cave. Do not return if you're very brave.' She suddenly flew away again without a word.

I found a black cave - the ring still on my finger. I jumped into the fiery hole - it went black again.

A long time later my eyes slowly opened to find lots of coffins lying on the floor, dead trees and rusty chains everywhere. The sky was rich red and the soil was dark brown. Without a word, I could tell this place was Hell.

Curiously, I explored this place high and low, only to find a devil.
He grumpily said, 'Go, go to the big black caves, say goodbye and wave!'
I was now petrified as I jumped into the black cave.

I opened my eyes again to find God sitting in a dark room. I had a very long talk with him until I said I wanted to go home.
'You can't,' he exclaimed, 'you're dead!'

Laura Hamer (12)
Sutton High School, Sutton

A Day In The Life Of A Chestnut Tree

Once again, the sun arises to mark the break of day and the town slowly begins to wake. As I am standing, where I have always stood, at the end of my road, looking down upon it, I wonder what the day will bring.

Day after day I stand here, watching the passers-by. Many of them make use of the facilities I have to offer. Many squirrels enjoy living with me because of my delicious chestnuts. I also have regular tenants of many different species of birds, including multicoloured sparrows and finches. Not forgetting the humans who make good use of me for shade.

Over the years that I have spent standing at the end of my road, I have witnessed many changes, changes which have helped man, but ruined nature.

I remember as a young sprout, I used to stand in the middle of the field in an area full of countryside. Next to me stood my two best friends, Blossom and Maple. We would stand together and enjoy the wind rippling through our hair, the rain washing us clean and the sun drying us up.

But then it all changed. While Blossom was young and small, the farmer dug her up and moved her a couple of fields down. Maple's fate was absolutely horrendous. They cut him down into tiny pieces and carried him away in a truck. I felt hollow.

Although my friends have gone, life still carries on.

Nivedita Chakrabarti (13)
Sutton High School, Sutton

A Day In The Life Of A Cat

Dear Kitty,

I think I'm in love!

I bet you're wondering what I'm going on about aren't you? Well I'll tell you then.

It all started when I was on my daily stroll across the neighbourhood, as I'm head of Neighbourhood Watch (we have a rat problem). Like I was saying, I strolled across the next-door's fence, looking as marvellous as usual, with my long, sleek, black coat and my white face. Josie, my mummy, calls me Sylvester sometimes, you know, from that silly cartoon where the cat always misses the bird. That's not like me, I brought in three birds last week! I laughed but Josie was grumpy as she had to take them out.

I always swish my tail at Josie's sister, Emily, but I like Josie, she remembers to feed me, though sometimes she doesn't turn the tap on for me to drink.

Anyway, I heard Susan, Josie's mum, shake the food container. Yum, that means breakfast! I ran through my cat-flap then . . . I saw her. She was treading nervously around the wooden floor.

Richard, Josie's dad, picked me up. He's quite rough so I didn't struggle. He told me that Emily thought I was a bit lonely, so she had bought me a friend. Maybe I should like Emily more than Josie now? Nah, impossible!

I found out her name . . . Amber! Beautiful! Hang on, what's that sound? She's coming up the stairs! I have to go.

Josephine Rawes (12)
Sutton High School, Sutton

A Day In The Life Of A Victorian Peasant Girl

Lucy is a Victorian peasant and lives in one room of a slum with her four younger siblings and her ill mother.

Dear Diary

Thank goodness today is over. It was rent day and we had to give our last few coins to pay so we have no money and I don't get paid until the end of this week. Bethany needs more clothes and Mum needs to see a doctor, or at least have some decent food. Alas, we can't afford either. Tom will have to scavenge at the factory, even though it's dangerous to have to be under the machines all the time and even though he's only eight, that's the only way we're going to get the money. Oh how I wish Father was still around or that Mother was better. It's so difficult looking after three growing children, a sick mother and pay the rent all on one very poor salary.

Yes, Tommy will have to work. I don't know who will look after Beth and Michael while we're gone. Mother certainly can't watch them, she can't do anything, so she can't help. Michael's only five, he can't look after a three-year-old. I suppose he's going to have to. I'll have to send Tom out begging.

I have clothes to patch. Some of our clothes are so old they have patches on the patches. If only we had some money, we might have a decent life. Oh well, we'll just have to make do.

Louise Privett (12)
Sutton High School, Sutton

THE MURDEROUS RIVER

It was a scorching day. The sun beamed down on the shore of the Amazon. This was the perfect day for canoeing.

The party heaved the canoes into the water one by one and in twos, jumped in excitedly. Eventually Jenny and I were the only ones left standing on the deserted beach. We exchanged glances and hopped into the canoe, grinning and laughing.

It was mid July and I was on a month's adventure camp with my best friend, Jenny. 'It's so hot,' I groaned. I knelt down and ran my fingers through the cool water, but to my horror my foot caught onto something large. I tripped and plunged into the water head first.

I felt the water whoosh past me. I was sinking. I could not swim and my life jacket was in the canoe. I was going to put it on a few minutes into the journey downstream. The lifejacket was big and bulky. I thought I would become very sweaty if I wore it the whole time.

I could feel the pressure of hundreds of gallons of water above me. A surge of pain swept through my body. My eyes went out of focus and my lungs were screaming for air. Feeling dizzy, I closed my eyes.

'Claire,' I heard a faint voice call from far away. I opened my eyes. Everything was blurred, but I could just make out Jenny's lips form a smile. Warmth filled my body. I was alive!

Fiona Cooper (11)
Sutton High School, Sutton

A Day In The Life Of A Wolf

In the shadows of the Sucathian Mountains a fierce pack of wolves desperately seek shelter from the vicious, crisp winter.

A mysterious legend of survival and power, has been created about wolves and will cling to them until they become extinct from this planet.

It is an icy night in the country long ago known among the local people as Corromaia. The frosty ground creaks as the wolves scowl around, lurking in gloomy caves within the jagged rocks of the mountains.

As dusk arrives, a piercing howl is heard from miles away in the distance. The wolf pauses in her tracks, her ears twitching, her breath belting out of her mouth like smoke from a bonfire. However, it is her beady, terrifying eyes that speak of danger before her, not her howl.

A wild beast roams the land in front of her, a beast she had always been afraid of. Her eyes glisten in the twilight as she glares at the moon shining at her. The wolf builds up confidence as if the moon itself had guided her through this difficult situation.

Quick as a flash, the wolf bounds towards the stray beast and begins tormenting it in the fear of her life. Her fierce opponent, now and again, gives swift bites on the wolf's back, but proves to be weaker. The beast soon surrenders and deserts the wolf. Her distant pack gives a long bay in honour of their everlasting acquaintance.

Victoria Hallam (12)
Sutton High School, Sutton

A Day In The Life Of A Dog

Woof, woof! Hi-ya, I'm Sasha and I'm a cocker spaniel dog! My owner always tells me how easy my life is but sometimes it can be hard! I mean, isn't there a saying, *it's a dog's life* - that's not fair! Well take today - wee li'l me gets very tired!

I'm walking now, round and round in my basket you see, because I'm trying to find the right comfy place! Anyway, then in comes my owner, who looks at me and starts laughing! I mean, what's so funny about that? I mean, I can tell you many funnier things that my owner does! For example: (Guess what he does!) He watches something with things moving inside it and it has sounds coming out of it (I think it's called an *elevillion* or something like that) anyway I think that's funny! I mean, watching the other thing with clothes (something that humans wear) in it is way better! It's actually interesting and exciting, though it does make your eyes go funny. It goes round and round and I do get dizzy! Ha, ha! (I was watching it a few minutes ago!)

After my long nap, I finally get up and walk around the room for a stretch. I am a little itchy so I am just going to roll over and over on my spiky mat! Ahh! Lovely! My owner should take me for walkies! I'd better let him know and get my lead!

Laughing *again,* (I don't know why. How else would I let him know?) he takes me for walkies and when I get back I'm very tired! I go back into my basket and you see, what a hard, hard d-d-day! Zzzzzzzzz.

Carla Busso (12)
Sutton High School, Sutton

A Day In The Life Of A Frock

Entry 1:
Hi ya, I'm Pinky, I'm a pink frock and I live in Marks & Spencer, it's dead posh, well at least for me! Oh no. I'm getting sold to a big, fat, ugly lady (well, I think she's a lady - she looks more like a monster). I've spent my whole life here and I'm already getting sold. I'm only a week old. Unfair!

Entry 2:
Hi again, this is the first time I've ever been worn properly, it's so exciting. I'm a bit tight for her but never mind.

We're driving to a fancy place now. Mrs Cook's husband is wearing a big hat and a suit. I must say they look ever so smart. *Wow!* A horse and carriage with a beautiful lady in it. She's wearing a wonderful, white frilly dress.
'Hi.' Oh, she can't hear me. I bet she's a lovely dress.

We're going into the church now. It's very nice. There's the dress again and the lady, she's walking down the aisle. Now they've agreed to be husband and wife. It's raining inside - weird. Wait, it's Mrs Cook's crying. I know it's touching but there's no need to soak me!

Entry 3:
Goodness me. She's a messy eater! Oh, at least I get some wedding cake. It's a pink iced cake with a thick layer of cream and jam. Yum, yum and extra yum.

Entry 4:
This is the most interesting day ever and I've just realised *I love cake.* Now I am extremely sorry to say this is my last entry.

Wajeeha Ahmed (11)
Sutton High School, Sutton

A Day In The Life Of Some Wedding Flowers

Hi, I'm called Crumply. Here I am sitting in freezing cold water, with leaves falling off me. I am so ugly, but all the other flowers are so pretty and colourful. I really want to get sold. I've sat here all my life, and still haven't managed to be sold!

Wow, a beautiful young lady is buying me! I can't believe it. I've never even been looked at before and now suddenly I'm being bought! I heard my owner's name is Justine and she is 22 years old. Perfect age! They've treated me so well, I've even got some of my colour back! I'm so glad that that they bought me!

Today is the big day! *The wedding day*! I've been waiting for this day all my life! Now, out of the middle of nowhere, it has finally come! *Jing-a-ling-a-ling,* the wedding bells ring. I'm coming down the aisle! This is so scary! What a relief, it is over now! I love these people, they've been so good to me recently, and it's been the most amazing week in my life!

Aarrgghh, I'm getting chucked behind Justine. I wonder who is going to catch me? I hope I get into the hands of a lovely, beautiful lady like Justine! *Ouch!* They're pulling me about everywhere, now I'm on the floor and all I can see is people running up to me, trying to get me! One thing's for sure, I look like all the rest of the flowers now!

Priyanka Amin (11)
Sutton High School, Sutton

A DAY IN THE LIFE OF MILLI THE CAT!

6.45am: Daddy comes down to give me breakfast, although he *never* does it properly. As soon as I'm done, I shoot off upstairs to lie on Kathryn's bed. She appreciates me.

8.15am: I have the whole house to myself, just how I like it. I can run about everywhere, and do whatever I want. I have a ball!

1pm: Time to go on my daily adventure, which usually takes about three hours. I go all sorts of places, to the local park, to other people's gardens. I go wherever I please, and do whatever I want. I have no responsibilities.

4pm: Kathryn and Lucy come home about now. They make a *huge* fuss of me and they call me stupid names like 'Tinker' and 'Dan'! What an enjoyable life I have! They always fight over who loves me the most.
'She's *my* cat,' says Lucy.
'I feed her!' says Kathryn. I wish they'd shut up, it's pretty obvious who I like most and that's Kathryn. She feeds me, cuddles me, and is kind to me. She's my favourite.

10pm: Kathryn and Lucy go to bed about now. This is when the fighting really starts. It's great entertainment! The problem is, I end up like a swing, going backwards and forwards from their bedrooms, as they both want me on their bed. I end up sleeping downstairs and waking up again in the morning, time to do it again. It's a cat's life!

Kathryn Griffiths (12)
Sutton High School, Sutton

MY IMAGINARY FRIEND

I hated myself. Spots. Skinny legs. Ugly face. Have you ever hated yourself so much? But I was lucky because if Elizabeth hadn't been in my dreams, I would have had a lonely life.

Elizabeth was my imaginary friend and she taught me how miserable my life would be if I hated myself. When I went upstairs starting to sleep I had a horrible dream. Elizabeth was in the dream trying to persuade me that if I kept on thinking my way I would always be gloomy.

As I walked into a dark, dull room of my dream, I saw a small woman crying and looking out of the window. I moved closer and closer towards the figure. As I approached, I asked her, 'Why are you crying?'
'Well as you have seen me, this will be you in the future but it's not too late if you change your mind you will have a better life. If you don't change your mind you will be just like me. I am warning you!'
I didn't know what to do when I heard these words. I was scared.

Next morning, I woke up and thought about the words she said to me. After that I changed my mind and I no longer hated myself.

When I think back at those lonely days, I realise that Elizabeth had had a positive effect on me. Being alone is a sad life, but she taught me that living is a wonderful thing. I realise that now, I wish I had realised it earlier.

Seong Won Cha (12)
Sutton High School, Sutton

A Day In The Life Of Ginger (My Pet Fish)

I was looking out at the glorious sea, all my friends who were also called Ginger, were swimming through the reeds.
'Argh!' I was being dragged up in a net; Ginger and Ginger were coming too!
'Nnnooooooooo!'
I howled, only bubbles erupting from my mouth. It was no use; I was leaving my home in the Caribbean Sea.
'I'm choking!' wailed Ginger my eldest sibling. True enough we left the sea and were dying. We were being transported to England.

Now in England, I swam in my large tank. I'd been here for almost a month and no one had picked me. Suddenly a girl, tallish with red hair walked past me. I looked disappointed once again.

Two weeks passed and more people had walked past.
'Wait, look Ginger, a curly haired girl,' I shouted excitedly.
'Oh no, she walked straight past,' I whispered sadly, as she sauntered along. I swam drearily to my castle.
'Hey stop that! Oh no not again.'
Once again, I was being lifted out from my home but this time it was only me! I was going home at last.

The next three years of my life were great, I was swimming with my new friends, Rocky, Pebbles, Bam-Bam and Dino.

Alexandra San Miguel-Brathwaite (12)
Sutton High School, Sutton

A Day In The Life Of A Postage Stamp

A hand reached out to grab me and removed me from the booklet of ten. I was stuck onto an envelope and shoved into someone's trouser pocket.

I was taken into the car and after a few moments of driving, the vehicle stopped at a red cylindrical object at the side of the road.

In no time at all, I found myself inside the postbox. The door suddenly opened and the postman collected the letters and parcels and stuffed them all into one bag.

We were loaded onto a lorry where there were several other sacks and when we had arrived at the post office, we were carried, sack by sack, into the building. The contents of the sacks were sorted into different categories, according to our final destinations.

Soon afterwards, I was thumped by several ink stamps and put into another sack and bundled on top of a large pile of luggage on a plane. It was very uncomfortable, as there were lots of parcels, which were big enough to squash you.

The plane began to move and within eight hours, I had arrived at the sorting office in Sri Lanka. From there, I was delivered by bicycle to a house in Jaffna and handed over to a little girl, who seemed very excited.

My letter was ripped open and inside was a birthday card from her favourite aunt in England. The great smile on her face made me glad that I had been used for a good cause.

Saranya Ravindran (12)
Sutton High School, Sutton

A Day In The Life Of Air

On Saturday I was floating around, passing all the shops when I suddenly was sucked downwards by a man. He had brown hair and he had a big rough beard. His hair was very long. He smelt funny but I had smelt worse. I got sucked into his mouth. That smelt even more. My best friend Francesca had been sucked in as well. Laura, Lisa and Harriette were pulled into a pretty, young girl. She looked about 10. They always get the nice people.

Inside his throat there were a lot of bones sticking out. He may be fat on the outside, but there was not much on the inside. I do enjoy sliding down into the heart, it's like a roller coaster ride. I hate it in the heart though. All of the hearts that I have met have been bullies to me. They never let me go on the full roller coaster ride around the whole body, I only get to try the demo. This heart was especially mean to me. He weighed me on the machine and said that I was a reject. Then with his powerful thump, I went shooting out, up the throat, in the smelly mouth, this time when I was passing up, I hit myself a few times on some chips going the other way, and out back into the street.

Harriette, Lisa and Laura were a long time. They had obviously been accepted, then I got dragged down again - oh great.

Katherine Dart (11)
Sutton High School, Sutton

LIFE

Every day has its obstacles to pass. Some big or small, and some hard or easy. This is not the case for me as life itself is one big obstacle that one day I will finally and hopefully achieve.

The continuous meetings about schooling, improvements, health care and everything and anything. I put a brave face on to try not to show that I'm petrified. The world doesn't understand that I am a normal person who is lumbered with questions and problems, I've got to make one choice and that choice is what I think is best for everyone.

Every move I make, every word I say millions of people watching me, staring, wondering what I am going to do next. After the statements I feel relived like boulders have been taken off my shoulders which have been sitting there for hours; but when I wake up and collect the newspaper from my doorstep I feel the exact same as before. Everywhere statements, reviews all about me, all bad.

I want to know where people get these accusations from, they can't really think they are true? I'm losing people's trust, mainly because of the media, and that's not good when you have to make people like and trust you with their lives.

The most irritating and most upsetting aspect of being me is that my family are getting affected, bullied and judged. Well, these are the consequences you have to pay to be Prime Minister.

Aarani Sundaram (13)
Sutton High School, Sutton

CASTLE ON C9

I wake every morning in my soft bed to see the glorious sunshine filtering through my curtains. The birds sing in elation whilst the sensation of summer and the comfort of safety envelop my mind. As I tread downstairs I pass a mirror and see a twenty-one-year-old, carefree person, despite the fact that I am several years older, I walk into an open plan kitchen and find cupboards full of food. The feeling of well-being calms me, as it does each and every day and I breakfast whilst looking out onto the rest of C9.

Later on, as I travel to my workplace, I contemplate how perfect my life is; I have a job that I dreamt about when I was younger and which pays excellently as well. My network of friends extends all over the world. My parents live in a villa in Spain whilst my sister has a husband and two wonderful children. My family have been on the National Rich List for seven generations and I'm marrying my childhood sweetheart next month. I have a busy social and work life but always find time to sit back and reflect. I have degrees in 21 different subjects ranging from dance to quantum physics. I have found my inner self. There is no dictatorship, war, drought, famine or racism because everyone on Cloud 9 is at peace with themselves.

This is my legendary life. I am a myth.

Mei-Lian Hoe (13)
Sutton High School, Sutton

UNTITLED

That night the wood was dark and the only light came from the moon. Jenny thought that this was the end!

He was standing there, his eyes filled of hatred. Jenny who was sitting down in a huddle where John had thrown her, she was shaking with fear. What would he do to her?

John who had sweat dripping off his forehead suddenly looked around to see if there was a spade. As he was doing so Jenny started biting frantically at the rope which was getting her nowhere.

The shadows started spinning and Jenny started sweating and throwing herself to the ground and yelling, *'Get me out of here!'*

At this John came over and started kicking her and saying she was going to die and no one could help her. Jenny being only 13 and not knowing much about life started yelling again until John put the knife to her throat and told her to be quiet.

As the night went on John started becoming impatient and restless so John decided he would start digging a grave for Jenny. John had great enjoyment knowing that he was going to kill someone and get away with it. Where as Jenny wasn't feeling so happy, in a figure of speech.

A car could be heard driving into the wood, could this be help for Jenny? All that she knew was that John started to look worried and nervous, he suddenly rushed over to Jenny and . . .

Gemma Winters (13)
Sutton High School, Sutton

A Day In The Life Of A Lift Operator

It's a simple life. I sit on a stool in the lift of Beamsly's department store. 'Which floor?' I ask.

'Haberdashery,' the lady in the green woollen coat mumbles into her scarf. I press the button for the third floor, musing that these days very few people even know what haberdashery is.

They used to give the job of lift operator to someone with one leg or an undefined war injury. I have as many limbs as the next man, so you may wonder how I got the job.

First, though, I should tell you why I like it. All day, people ask me questions. 'Which floor for the toy department?'
I reply: 'Fourth.' Simple question, simple answer, happy customer: each human need satisfied instantly at the touch of a button. Does any other job in this complex world provide such a straightforward public service?

The lift is a world of its own: warm, dry and hospitable. I am content to be the almost unnoticed host. Outside, the world rolls on without me. In my lift, there is no day or night, and the only sign of the weather is when chilly customers shuffle in, stamping snow from their boots, or flicking wet strands of bedraggled hair from their faces.

My lift, you ask? Indeed, for like the whole store, it was left to me by my father. Why should the wealthiest man in town not enjoy a simple pleasure?

Jessie Cowan (12)
Sutton High School, Sutton

THE RED CEILING

The ceiling was red. That was my first thought when I opened my eyes. The thick blackness, which had been the background to my mind, had been replaced with a bright red, and muttered chatter infiltrated the deathly silence that had stifled my thoughts.

I didn't wonder where I was, for when you've been in the sort of unpleasant place that I have been in, then it's quite sufficient to know you're out of there.

I was, however, interested in why I was there, but as I tried to turn my head I was blocked, this bed was highly restricting, limiting my view to the ceiling. However, it was extremely comfortable, I could have lain among the silken sheets forever.

My thoughts turned to the familiar cream ceilings of home and the music, which penetrated every corner of our house. There was music here, but not the sort of music that I enjoyed, this music was decidedly grim.

All my thoughts were disjointed, like a broken videotape, my memories were all muddled and suddenly I felt exhausted with life.

The talking, which had been as regular as the music, stopped abruptly and the first few bars of my favourite song played. It was almost as if they knew I was coming. Then I felt myself being lifted, 'Excuse me!' I said loudly. No one heard. 'I said *stop!*' I screamed.

Nobody reacted at all but then why should they? They had never listened to me when I was alive.

Louise Hanger (13)
Sutton High School, Sutton

THE CRASH

I was cutting through the air at an indescribable speed, with the cold wind screaming past me, stabbing at my body like knives. I found time to look down at the land rushing past below me and I caught my breath with the sheer beauty of it. Green forests covered the area like a blanket, but there were gaps large enough to see sparkling blue rivers cutting through them. The exhilaration of flying a fighter plane in a full-scale battle is something that has to be felt to be believed.

With German planes speeding towards me from all sides, the only way that I could go was down. I nose-dived at such a speed that I was practically free falling. My stomach leapt into my mouth, my heart was drumming in my chest and if it weren't for my goggles, the cold air rushing past would have blinded me. The 'Jerries' weren't stupid enough to follow me and soon tired of the chase, pulling away to terrorise another young volunteer pilot.

I was so preoccupied with the action behind me that for a split second I lost my concentration and tried, without success, to pull out of my spiralling dive. I wasn't dizzy; somehow planes always seem to defy the laws of gravity. With the engine roaring like an angry lion, I brushed the treetops with my wings and I knew that there was no way out. I was going to crash . . .

Katie Buckhalter (13)
Sutton High School, Sutton

A Day In The Life Of A Victim

My nightmare had woken me again. I was sweating, short of breath. My body shook as I got out of bed. It seemed so real, exact to every detail, I didn't like to contemplate about it. At least I knew today he could be locked away, I might be able to put my mind at rest.

It was eleven by the time I'd readied myself, it wasn't just getting changed, I had mental exercises that my psychiatrist had given me, they helped me to face the exterior world. When it first happened, I couldn't stand it out there, everything had betrayed me, but I was now regaining my trust. 'Everything will be fine, everything will work out,' I chanted, leaving the house.

I stood in the box, I gave evidence. It wasn't enough, I wanted to say more, I wanted to burst out, but I couldn't. He was there. He stood up to testify. His words were lies and deceit, yet he was so believable. I had to do something, I had to protest. My head spun, it was all too much.

I heard machines and people. My eyes opened, hospital again. There was a card to my side.
'Get better soon, sorry to hear that your case fell through, another time maybe. Love Mum.'
Oh please no, I can't live with him out there, I'd been betrayed again, it was just too hard. My head hurt. Everything went black.

Deborah Farr (14)
Sutton High School, Sutton

A Day In The Life Of A Book

Sitting on a shelf in a bookshop, crammed together so I couldn't breathe. Lots of other books identical to me were lined up next to me.

Then all of a sudden a hand took hold of me and lifted me up. It was a young and small hand. It bent back my cover to read the first page. I looked up to see it was a face of a small girl. Her eyes were darting across the page, reading the words printed there. The hand closed the book and turned me over so the girl could read the back. As soon as she had read it, I felt myself banging against her leg.

I was placed on a cold, smooth surface. Another pair of hands picked me up, they were bigger than before. A red light came down on me and I heard a deafening beep. I was put into a plastic bag and given back to the little girl. I was jostled around in the bag and bumped against a leg, yet again, as I was carried home.

Finally I was taken out of the bag. I was opened up again and I could see the girl reading my pages. She kept on reading until she had finished the first chapter. Then this strip of paper was put between my pages, it felt funny and it tickled. Then I was dropped onto a chair.

I was owned, I would bring lots of fun, learning and enjoyment to my owner forever.

Esther Nicoll (12)
Sutton High School, Sutton

THE GIRLS' BRIGADE

I stood, scrutinising the group of girls at the other end of the playground, or the Girls' Brigade as everybody called them. I'd only been in London for two weeks and I already knew that everybody wanted to be in the Girls' Brigade, mainly because Lucinda was the richest girl at Mitcham School. She was covered in designer labels; I glanced back down at my tatty old hand-me-down shirt and scruffy jeans. The Girls' Brigade started walking over to me.

'Listen Sarah, do you want to be in the Girls' Brigade?' Lucinda said boldly with a grin like a Cheshire cat.
I looked abruptly at my best friend Nicole, who stared back at me blankly. I nodded at Lucinda gingerly. What was the catch?
'On one condition, you ditch that geeky Nicole girl.'
Ditch Nicole? She was my best friend, but I could become part of the Girls' Brigade.
'Um . . . I guess.' What had I just said? What about Nicole?
'Go on then.' She turned to Nicole and began to pick on her, then prompted me to say something to Nicole.
'I . . . guess so. I . . . mean.' I looked at Nicole; tears were running down her face.

What was more important, being part of the Girls' Brigade or being friends with Nicole? I ran back to Nicole. 'I'm sorry,' I said quietly. She turned away as if she couldn't hear me. I tried again.
Nicole turned around and looked me in the eye. 'Promise me that you'll never do it again.'
'I promise.'

Sana Sheikh (11)
Sutton High School, Sutton

ANNUAL CONGREGATIONAL MEETING

It's the Annual Congregational Meeting tomorrow. I'm dreading it. It's just so *boring*. Sitting there for two hours, trying to stay awake for the whole damned thing.

Mrs Canapé will be bulldozing down the aisle, shoving soggy digestives in people's faces. Mr Hammond will be rushing around, red-faced, adjusting the PA system and flicking switches. Mr Pond will be sitting at the front looking fat, apologising for people who were sensible enough not to bother turning up, and then droning on about how well the church is doing, how super the hall looks now Mrs Pledge has rearranged the flowers and how nice it was of Mrs Apron and Mrs Cakebread to do the tea bar.

Then there'll be the elections for new jobs, which is so unutterably *boring*. It takes *ages* to do because ninety per cent of the congregation are about five hundred years old and it takes them that long to raise their hands. Then the votes are counted and finally Mr Pond stands up, straightens his tie, nods to Mr Hammond to turn his microphone up extra loud, and booms something about who the next church warden is, who the next church gardener is, who's going to be tidying the Bibles after services and everything down to the most minuscule and pointless of things.

I really don't know why I go. It's so distressingly tedious that I come out wanting to kill myself immediately.

But I suppose people expect me to be there. After all, I am the vicar.

Becky Mayhew (18)
Tolworth Girls' School, Sutton

YOU CAN RUN BUT YOU CAN'T HIDE!

I arrived on the coach at 'Camp Michigan.' All I could think about was that thrilling story I was told about the forest we were going to camp in. The bit that stuck out the most was when a child walked into the forest and was lost, then her compass spun around like a helicopter. Frightening isn't it?

Anyway no point worrying about that now, we are already here. The teachers gave out compasses and called out the cabin numbers and who was put in which cabin, as I prayed not to be with my worst enemies Frankie, Niomie and Tara. Miss called out my name 'Paris,' then called Frankie, Niomie and Tara. Great!

'No I want the top bunk!'
There was an argument as soon as we arrived at our cabin, so why don't we put names in a hat? I suggested. Then they all shouted at me telling me that I would be the last person to choose where to sleep so I held back and went out for a walk in the forest to clear my head.

Thoughts ran through my mind like those phrases from that haunting story. Night came quickly as I looked up at the dark sky, then ahead of me at the deep, dark and eternal forest. It was time for me to go back, I turned around to walk back and the path was gone so I looked at my compass, it told me the way to go, well kind of. It started to spin around like a helicopter, just like the child in that story so I ran one way (east) . . . then another (west) . . . then another (south) . . . and there was only one way left to go, north, so this time I walked. Then I realised I wasn't alone.

Thoughts again ran across my mind like a cheetah as I was so confused and there was one thought that slithered across my mind slowly like a snail leaving a trail of fear in my mind. Then I could hear a quiet voice say, 'Don't be afraid you're never alone,' and I could hear it getting louder and *louder* so I ran towards the trees. Then dropped to the ground.

I got up slowly and walked around hearing screaming topping that haunting voice so I looked to my right and I could see a man burying a black body next to a young girl screaming and oddly there was a name plate beside the burial and you wouldn't believe it, my name was on it (Paris Chere Jones). My heart skipped a beat and I held in my scream and turned to my left but I was caught! Knocked out!

I woke up, I opened my eyes and there was mud being thrown on my face. I was in a hole in the ground. I was being buried. I couldn't do anything about it, my head was loaded with that haunting voice and a flashback of my life as I slowly passed away.

Latoya Walker (14)
Walthamstow School For Girls, Walthamstow

ALONE

Some people believe when people die they go to Heaven, others don't .

It was a cold, dark night. Symone wrapped her coat around her as the cold whipped around her pinching, her flesh. She and her mum had fought for the last time, she was running away from home. 'I just want to be alone.'

Suddenly she bumped into a sharp, bony figure. When she looked up she saw he was cloaked in black and a shadow cast upon his face. She stepped past him, he stayed dead still. She looked round, he was still there. When she turned around again he was gone but when she turned back he stood in front of her. She hastily stepped into the road. Suddenly a lorry burst around the corner. The blinding light cut through the fog, the horn roared, the tyres screeched.

Symone sat bolt upright in bed. It was just a dream. She stared into the darkness. Her hand fumbled for the light switch, she turned it on. It immediately snapped off. Then it started flickering, a mirror was hurled across the room and shattered into a thousand pieces. 'Mum help,' she screamed.
Her mum walked in, she stared wide-eyed into the room. She looked at the bed Symone was lying in and calmly flicked the light switch and walked out.
'Mum?' Symone murmured. 'She must still be angry with me,' she pulled back the bed covers and ran after her.

Symone found her at the kitchen table, staring into space. 'Mum the mirror . . . it moved, it smashed itself, there's a ghost!'
Her mum just sighed and shook her head.
'You don't believe me do you?'
Her mum remained silent.

Symone stormed out, ran into the front room and wept. An eerie draft blew through her hair, the window banged and the light began to flicker. Then the figure from her dream appeared at the window and vanished. She frantically dialled 999 but the line seemed dead.

The door slammed open, the cloaked figure stood there. Symone raced past it, up the stairs, screaming. She ran into a cupboard. She slammed the door behind her and crumpled into the darkness of the corner. Her sweaty hands pressed against the wall. She didn't want to die. She heard footsteps approach. Why would no one help her? Why would no one answer the scream?

Suddenly the footsteps stopped. Symone jumped to her feet and grabbed the handle, which twisted vigorously in her hands, blood now trickled down her fingers. Suddenly the handle turned, she snapped back and crumpled into the corner. The door crept open, light poured in revealing the dark shadowed figure. Symone cringed, huddled up. This was surely it. The figure pushed her aside and pointed. Symone turned her head. A grave!

Symone Smith
1988-2002
Killed by lorry
Loved and missed

So she was killed by the lorry, and the figure, the figure was death. 'All I wanted was to be alone, now I am, forever . . .'

Mariam Olayiwola (14)
Walthamstow School For Girls, Walthamstow

THE MISUNDERSTANDING

The shining full moon took over the cloudless sky. The trees were rustling and wailing. I was hurrying through the forest to get to my home. I could only hear the crunching of the autumn leaves under my feet. The wind was howling violently. My hair was everywhere. My spine shivered. I looked around me to find that I was all alone. What little did I know that my life would never be the same?

I never felt comfortable living in that house by myself. My father went on a business conference in Italy for a few months. My mother was dead and I was an only child so there was no one to look after me. My new best friend Jezebel made me feel comfortable in this new town, but not that comfortable. I got these very bad dreams quite often. I'd always see a muffled picture of three people in a car; I could always hear screams, shrieks and shouting. Then I'd hear a loud bang. I always woke up at this point because I always got scared.

For my birthday Jezebel gave me a photo frame which I put in my bedroom. I went into my front room to watch a little TV and found that my photo frame was on top of my TV. I thought I was imagining it but I must have misplaced it, I told myself. I went to sleep that night thinking I was crazy. When I woke up that morning I was shocked to find that my photo frame was back in my bedroom. Now I knew I was definitely insane.

For a couple of days nothing happened but one night I was trying to call some friends of mine to come over, but no one answered. After a couple of hours Jezebel answered, she came round but she seemed very distant and kept herself to herself. She wasn't the same funny person she always was. We were watching TV and we heard some screams. I thought that I was just imagining it but later we realised that it was real. I thought that my house was haunted. I quickly ran into my room and left Jezebel behind. Everything went silent. I stood by the door. I couldn't hear Jezebel. I was feeling scared for her. I quietly opened the

door and went into my father's room. I was whispering, 'Come here Jezebel.' I felt a tap on my shoulder, I looked round to find Jezebel as if she was in a car accident, I asked her, 'What happened to you?'
She replied, 'It's time you knew the truth.'
She pulled out a newspaper and it had a picture of me and Jezebel and another man dead. The headline was *People found dead in car crash.*

Mobeen Sultan
Walthamstow School For Girls, Walthamstow

A Day In The Life Of Me

I escaped to the safety of the vast, derelict space that was our attic. Originally sent to find the antique Christmas tree decorations, I decided to have a bit of a nose around.

I spluttered and coughed as a huge blast of dust flew in my nostrils. Although my eyes had become blurry and water, I managed to feel my way. From the corner of my eye, I caught a glimpse of something move. I gasped in surprise, my eyes grew wide as footballs, and my heart gave irregular beats. Acting stupidly I strode forward and fell slap-bang in the middle of an array of boxes and bags, which littered the rich, oak floor.

I stayed dumbstruck for a while, when I gathered what was left of my wits and courage, I went to look for this mysterious object. I ignored the violent beats my heart was giving. Determined to find out what it was, I edged nearer on my hands and knees. I hurried my pace and slowly with such cunningly I turned to face the attic demon.

I would have laughed out loud, if I weren't heaving a sigh of relief. The thing that had terrified me, was nothing more than a tacky piece of coffee stained paper. Hunching down, I grabbed the piece of sobbing paper, it read,
Do not read, take heed and beware
After completing this verse, you have much to fear
Awake will the thing nightmares derive from
The purest unknown evil, shall be free
It will seek the one being, who is its key
For now it's stuck between the worlds of living and dead
It will only rest, once it has taken the soul of that who said
This incantation and disturbed its peace.

The hairs on the back of my neck stood up, I began shivering continuously. My gut was telling me something big was about to happen. Suddenly the bathroom door slammed shut. My senses sharpened, every minute noise was picked up by my ears. Instantly, I was on my feet, the muscle in my jaw twitched. I gave quick constant glances backwards, each time my gut did somersaults gasped for breath, but I dare not stop, the perspiration kept flowing out from my pores.

I flung open the door, only to be greeted by a horrific sight. It was purely hideous, this ghoul wasn't white and friendly, but dark, dull and menacing. A low threatening hiss escaped from the hole in its face. I uttered a small cry of horror, before collapsing on the white floor. I clung my head, the pain inside was intense, I howled and groaned in despair, its gaze held my gaze. The mirror smashed, the small glittery shards flew into my eyes. I sobbed even louder, this was pain beyond anyone's imagination. I felt the blood gush out of my head as a heavy object, collided with the side of my skull.

Sophia Choudhry (14)
Walthamstow School For Girls, Walthamstow

GHOST STORY

Julie and Jacob were looking for a new house, so they visited a little cottage in a village nearby. The house was surrounded by ivy and there were small flower buds beginning to open on the front lawn. They opened the huge heavy door and looked around, it all seemed very lovely and beautiful so they decided to buy the house right away. On the night of their arrival they heard a tap at the door and they went to answer it. There standing behind the door was a girl about seven years old.
'Hello what can I do for you young lady?' asked Jacob.
'Sorry but my ball flew over the fence and I was wondering if I could have it back please?'
'Of course you can, come in and meet my wife Julie.' The girl followed Jacob inside and walked towards Julie.

'Hello I'm Clarice, I came to retrieve my ball back. By the way I'm going to the station later so could you ask your husband to hurry up please?'
'I know, why don't I give you a lift to the station myself?' asked Julie. Jacob came back carrying the ball in his hands.
'OK, that would be nice,
' said Clarice. They walked out of the house towards the house. Julie put her hand out and opened the back door of the car but when she turned around Clarice wasn't there.

The day after Julie came home looking very shocked. 'What's the matter Julie?' asked Jacob.

Julie told him that when she was at work today she was talking to her boss about how great it was that there was a train station in town, her boss looked at her as if she was mad and told her that there wasn't a train station nearby and that the last station closed down in 1910. Julie couldn't sleep that night and then she realised Clarice must have been a ghost.

From that day on Jacob and Julie could never sleep at night because they were scared that Clarice might come back and haunt them. No one knows what happened after that but all they knew was that Julie and Jacob died a very unusual death.

Rosa Dudley-Hibbett (12)
Walthamstow School For Girls, Walthamstow

FOLLOW THE BLOOD TRAIL

We were all chatting in our science class when our new science teacher came in. He looked OK and he was quite loud when he was taking the attendance. He called out my name twice, 'Alice?' he said loudly.
I was busy chatting to my friend. I answered, 'Yes Sir.' He looked at me suspiciously, like I knew something that I shouldn't know. From that time I knew that there was something about him that I should know but I didn't care much.

He had a very different way of describing blood vessels. He used the word *juice* in our lesson, which my friend and I thought was disgusting. The next day I went to his office to give him all the course work that we had done with the previous teacher. I was at the door about to enter his office. On his door he had his initials and his name which was really weird; *VB, Mr Vobdar Belson.* He was drinking this dark red liquid, quite like blood. But I thought, *it can't be!*

I came home from school and dad had cooked dinner. I had dinner and I looked at the calendar. It was my mum's birthday today. I had a little present for her which I put near her picture. I miss my mum, she died a year ago. At night I saw my mum's ghost telling me that I should not go to school, there was danger there for me. I went to school in the morning and told my friends about it. They said they wanted to investigate with me.

So we followed him after school. He went quite far and we lost track. Then we saw some blood drops on the road. We followed the drops, they led us to a room. We went in on the roof. There were lots of bats and as they flew out, we screamed. When the bats had gone we entered the room and looked up. We saw a big vampire bat. It looked too big to be a normal vampire bat. We were very scared and just ran home. The next day when we went to our science class we were scared but he didn't say anything. Then he started to tell us off for no reason. At the end of the lesson he told us to stay behind and said that he thought we were trouble.

We went out of the class and saw the bloody footsteps leading up to the principle's office. When we went into his room he jumped at us and threw the red drink over himself and he vanished. Our teacher was a mystery solved.

Everything turned out OK but our principle had to be changed. I hope our new principle is a good fairy.

Sara Akhtar (13)
Walthamstow School For Girls, Walthamstow

THE HAUNTED HOUSE

Nat and Greg sneaked quietly down the stairs. It was midnight. Mum and Dad would be asleep. Greg turned on the flashlight.
'OK' he said, 'waterproof jackets?'
'Check,' answered Nat.
'Gloves, camera, rucksack?'
'Check, check and check.'
'Great, then we're ready.'
'Right, OK' Nat said.
'Come on!' said Greg.T

They got the keys to unlock the door. Greg put the key in the lock and prayed that it wouldn't be very loud. Thankfully it wasn't and they went outside. It was cold and frosty. There was some snow on the ground.
'Right,' said Greg, 'you know the plan. Straight to the other side of town and then towards Mayflower House.'
'OK. Hope that no one sees us, everyone knows the *Kingston Blond* hair.'
'Yes, we'll have to hurry, come on. Dad leaves for work at five and it's half midnight.'

They ran out of the gate and onto the streets of Barkingway. They ran fast until they took a break for some tea. On they went until they reached Mayflower House. It was now deserted but had been inhabited by a number of families. It was said to be haunted by the ghost of a girl that had died there but no one had proved it. Greg wanted to be the one to prove whether it was true or not. They walked up the pathway and to the door.
'Ready?' asked Greg.
'Ready,' answered his sister nervously.

They pushed the dusty door and it creaked like it was in pain. They walked inside nervously and looked around.
'Wow!' said Nat. They were in a large hallway with a huge, moth-eaten rug on the floor. Around them hung pictures of stern-looking men, young girls and old women, all covered in dust and cobwebs. In one corner of the square room was an old, rusty suit of armour and an old,

carved staircase twisted its way up into the darkness above. There were three doors all leading to different rooms. All were closed.

'Let's go through that door,' Greg pointed to the door on his right.

His sister swallowed and spoke, 'OK then.'

They walked slowly towards the door and pushed it. Both of them jumped back and expected to see something scary. They opened their eyes and looked around.

'Not this door then,' joked Greg.

'Ha! Ha!' said Nat sarcastically. 'Let's try this one.'

They tried the other door and the same thing happened, nothing was in the room. They walked up to the last one.

'It has to be this door or it's upstairs,' said Nat.

'Yeah, scared little sis?' asked Greg.

'You wish,' she snapped back and pushed the door. It opened and there in the corner of the room was a ghost. A very vicious-looking ghost. A ghost who looked very vicious and was heading straight for them.

Katie Lewin (12)
Walthamstow School For Girls, Walthamstow

MY GHOST STORY

Andrew opened the front door to his new home with his newly married wife Sue in his arms. Andrew and Sue Reed had just got married that day. They couldn't wait to spend the rest of their lives together. Well, that's what Sue thought but in a very different way.

Andrew and Sue worked hard and got through everything that got in their way. They lived happily for many years but soon some news got to Sue which changed everything. Her friend told her that she had seen Andrew with a number of his friends and he was also with some young women, and they were doing more than just walking down the street. Her friend said that she followed Andrew and found him kissing one of the women.

Sue didn't know if she should believe her friend or not. So one night, when Andrew went out Sue followed him in her car. There were no girls, just five lads having a night out. But to make sure, Sue carried on. Sadly, around 12:30 the lads stopped walking and were standing around like they were waiting for someone. Soon three women met up with them. One wearing nearly nothing, walked up to Andrew. They hugged and then kissed. To Sue, the kiss was as long as time. She couldn't believe it. Why would he do this? Everything her friend said was true. Sue didn't want to stay any long, she was too hurt. She needed to get home before Andrew did anyway.

She got home and sat in the living room, thinking of what to say or do. Thinking about the kiss and the rat Andrew. She soon got an idea and went to the other room. Andrew had now come home. He walked in to see his wife standing there, her hand behind her back.
'Is there anything worrying you Sue?' Andrew said, knowing she knew something he didn't.
'Well yes there is,' Sue replied as she walked up to Andrew. Out of nowhere Sue pulled a sharp knife from behind her back and stabbed Andrew to death. She then buried the body in the garden.

For weeks no one found out about Andrew, but every night Sue had a nightmare of her killing Andrew over and over again. One night Sue was sitting upright in her bed, she had just had another nightmare. She looked around, it was dark and quiet. Suddenly a white light was heading right at her. She couldn't move. What could she do? The white light got faster and faster and then blew over Sue, making her fall back on her bed.

The light came down to Sue's face. It looked just like Andrew.
'You killed me, how could you?' Andrew said, 'I did one little thing wrong and this is how you get me back,' Andrew whispered.
'I didn't know what I was doing!' Sue cried.
Andrew's ghost moved away from Sue, who was shaking.
'I don't care any more, I just want to get even,' Andrew said. The ghost moved all around the house, up and down, making a mess wherever it went. It soon went back upstairs to where Sue was still shaking. In the same way he was killed by Sue with the knife, Sue was killed, a long and painful death. Now Sue and Andrew are both together, and it will be forever, in a place no one wants to go . . . Hell!

Emma Louise Pike (13)
Walthamstow School For Girls, Walthamstow

THE SALEM WITCH TRIALS

In the late 16th century there were many villages in America where the people were orthodox Christians. Everyone was expected to behave in a modest fashion. Often children rebelled. Some by dancing in forests, this was strictly forbidden.

These Christians were extremely superstitious. A few of the girls in the village started to behave strangely. More girls were influenced and they too behaved in a 'possessed manner'. Soon, women from the village were being accused of practising witchcraft and relating with the Devil. Seventeen people were hanged in Salem.

The characters' names are those who were involved in the Witch Trials. Some of the transcript has been taken from the original Salem Witch Trial records on the Internet.

'Let the Devil be upon you, let him wake and disturb your peaceful sleep. Nurse, you have pricked me and extracted my holy blood, replacing it with the Devil's.'
'Will someone please calm young Miss Abigail Williams. In our own court Rebecca Nurse, we have witnessed the sins you dare to commit, do not look me in the eye and repeat tales of your innocence,' the judge forcefully said.
'I can say I am innocent and God will hear my innocence.'
'Look Your Honour, he is standing there, his black shadow is cast upon your holy table, his breath is left on your neck. Aarrgghh, he pushes daggers of death in me to wound my soul.'
'Oh Abigail I feel him too, help me, I can't breathe.'
Abigail and Betty faint, leaving the focus of the trail to surround them.

Rebecca Nurse was convicted at 70 years of age for charges of practising witchcraft and was executed on Gallows Hill in Salem on July 19, 1692. Abigail William was 11 at the time of the trial.

It's over now; the priest has officially reported me, Abigail, and the other girls as without Devil. As if we nurtured the necessary ingredients to contain him in the first place. However, there are still a few pleading 'possessed.' I don't have the gloom of guilt rested upon my shoulders as many do. The memorable adrenaline pumping through my veins before each trial, overrules all guilt.

It's a dark night, no stars can be seen from my window. In the shadows of my bedroom, a figure could be seen. I couldn't see her face but I knew it was her, Rebecca Nurse. She surely would be seeking revenge. I wasn't frightened, I was hypnotised by her glow. It was like a soft, gentle fire dancing to a slow rhythm. Rebecca stepped towards me. My heart had stopped following a regular pattern. My delicate head was not safely upon my cushion; this was real.

'You seem to have forgotten,' Rebecca's unsteady voice said. She led me back a year to the execution. The streets we passed were empty; everyone was at Gallows Hill, I once again saw her climb the scaffold and then heard her neck break in two. The crowd's excitement once again echoed in my ears.

I was led back to the night when all the girls from the town danced around the fire. All the young girls were indulging themselves in the evening spirits.
'Higa-herti, Ab-suti, Higa-herti, Ab-suti.' The chants were muttered from all those dancing in the circle.

Suddenly from my young body, out rose a huge black shadow that entered the bodies of all the girls. I was the one in control. I was the one who made the girls cry in hysterics. I was meant for the rope. 'The Devil lives in me, I am drinking the innocent.' I turned to Rebecca. 'I have remembered my dark power. I hunger for the taste of blood to soothe my throat.'
Rebecca's eyes seared into mine. 'Leave Abigail's body and return with me to the underworld. We need you to sow the future seeds as you did in this witch hunt, when in times to come we wish men to shed the blood of their neighbours. You are the creator of all paranoia. But first, you must rest.'

Francesca Rothkell (13)
Walthamstow School For Girls, Walthamstow

CORRUPT, EVEN IN DEATH...

'It all started 200 years ago. The family who owned the manor house had just acquired a hunter, a huge chestnut named Glory. The youngest daughter, Elizabeth, was the first to ride him. He went so well, she decided to tackle the ditch. What she didn't know was that it had flooded during the night and the bank was slippery. She couldn't turn Glory in time and was trapped beneath him in the muddy water. They found their bodies in the morning.'

Laura finished. 'It's a good story isn't it? It did happen though, I found a reference in the library.'
'It's really scary, to think that ditch is still there,' replied Miranda. 'I suppose that's why we're not allowed to jump it.'
'Yeah, well I'm off, I've got to ride Goldie.' Abby left the small group gathered in the tack room.

The rain was lashing down outside, but if she rode around the edge of the lower paddock, the trees should shelter her a little.

Goldie started off as soon as Abby was in the saddle. 'That's strange, Goldie. You never leave the yard without a fuss.'

Goldie trotted onwards, heading towards the lower meadow without any direction from Abby. When they got there, he headed straight for the trees at the far end.
'Come on, under the trees where it's drier. The rain's getting worse,' Abby whispered.
Goldie turned away from the trees and started cantering towards the ditch.
'Slow down boy, where are you going? There's no way I'm jumping that thing. Stop, Goldie,' Abby pleaded with the horse as he sped up.
'Abby, what are you doing? You can't jump that!' Miranda shouted.

Then Abby realised. Goldie wasn't misbehaving; she was riding a different horse. In the dim evening light, she hadn't noticed the slightly darker colouring, or the lighter build. This horse was unlike any other in the yard. She had never seen it before.
'Abby, get off him now! You'll be killed!' Laura shrieked, running towards the ditch. 'Just get off him.'

Abby turned the horse in a tight circle. As he swung around, she jumped down, instinctively rolling clear. The horse took off, cleared the ditch and disappeared into the thick mist.

'Well, we'd better catch him. Your mum is not going to be pleased,' moaned Laura, pulling Abby to her feet. 'Come on, he'll be miles away by the morning.'

'Don't bother trying to find him Laura, he's not there,' called Abby, turning towards the stable block. 'It wasn't him I was riding. That wasn't even a real horse. That was a ghost.'

'Don't be stupid, how could it be?'

'Look, there are no hoof prints. There's where I fell off, and here's where he jumped. The ground should be all cut up . . .' Abby trailed off, staring at the spot where the horse had vanished. Along the edge of the ditch was written, 'I will return'. 'I think that was Glory. He was always corrupt, even in death . . .'

Merrila Cross (13)
Walthamstow School For Girls, Walthamstow

WHY ME?

I shivered as I waited in the gym at Walthamstow School For Girls, Walthamstow, for my after-school basketball lessons with Zara and my friends. I couldn't understand why they hadn't turned up yet; I mean I'd seen them all in the fifth period, so I couldn't figure it out. It was 4.15 and I was getting quite worried. I could hear strange noises; rustling and constant thuds, like something was creeping up behind me . . .

'Aarrgghhhhh!' I screamed, as I jumped out of my seat. I felt a cold, wrinkled hand touch my shoulder!

Suddenly, the lights went out. It was pitch-black and all I saw was the street lamps sneaking through the translucent windows. I began to stagger backwards, trying to find a door so that I could escape from whatever was going to happen. I heard loud crashes; it sounded like someone was racing around the place throwing everything onto the floor.

Bang!

My head hit the ground like a ton of bricks! I strained my eyes trying to open them. All I saw was a blur of ghostly basketballs. After lots of struggle, I slowly came to my feet. I turned around to see what had caused my fall. Darkness blocked my sight so I had to bend down to feel what it was. I picked up the 'object' it was a basketball. 'But it can't be!' I told myself. 'I didn't take one out and there wasn't one out when I got here!' My life went on standstill; something was wrong! I was being stalked!
'Cassie . . . Cassie . . . Cassie . . .' a croaky voice hissed. 'Watch out!'
I froze, I didn't know if I had heard correctly.
'Cassie . . . I'm coming to get you!' the voice growled.
'Leave me alone!' I stuttered.

I ran to the other side of the gym and found a door handle. I tugged at it as hard as possible, but it just wouldn't budge. I felt warm air blow on my face. All of a sudden, I was grabbed by the scruff of my T-shirt and raised a few feet off the ground. My face went red-hot, I couldn't breathe properly. I kicked and punched, trying to get away from this beast that wanted me dead!

'I've been after you for ages! And now I've got you! Ha! Ha! Ha!' the voice thundered.
I couldn't see anything! 'Help!' I squealed, trying to catch my breath.

Finally the 'voice' let me go; I crashed to the floor! I looked up; I saw a faint white figure float in front of me - I was terrified.
'You were always better than me at school. I hated you for it!' the voice bellowed. 'And when I died, you didn't care! I was so jealous of you, I still am, so now I'm going to get my own back!'
I put my hand over my mouth as the figure became clearer, 'Kevin . . .'

Saoirse Kennedy-Barton (12)
Walthamstow School For Girls, Walthamstow

ARE YOU THE NEXT GHOST?

I started to walk towards Samuel's house. We're in the same class, he's 14 years old, the same as me. I knocked on his front door. He came out and we walked to school. I had forgotten something, but I just couldn't remember.

I remembered what I had forgotten, it was my good luck ring. It's black, with a spider and has a green diamond on it.

On the way home, Samuel and I walked through the cemetery. We noticed a mausoleum, we hadn't ever seen it before; next to it was a marble carved face of a girl. It also had some writing next to it, it said, *Please help me, I want to live. Kiss me once, please kiss me.*
Samuel dared me to kiss the marble face of the girl. I kissed her lips. The lips were warm.

Suddenly, it became windy; the trees started rustling and the ground shook. There was a small wooden house that hadn't been open for years. It was dull and broken. The door slowly opened. She was the same girl whose face had been carved on the marble. She slowly came walking towards me; she was wearing old, dirty and ripped clothes and had a pale, white face. She said, 'My name is Hannah, could you help me? Could you kill a fly in that house?'
I said, 'No.'
Then she said, 'If I make you invisible, will you help me?'
We agreed.
'You'll be invisible from sunrise till sunset, but you'd better come back to me after sunset.'

The next day when I woke up, I was invisible. It was so much fun in school, I didn't even forget my spider ring. When I got to school I pulled the teacher's chair before she sat down, then I pulled some students' chairs and scribbled on some people's work that I didn't like.

At lunch I bumped into something, it was Samuel, he was invisible too. We went to the cemetery after sunset and were visible again. Hannah was there, she said, 'You had promised me that if I made you invisible, you would fight that fly in the house.'

I said, 'OK,' and went inside. There were many rooms in the house. At last I found the room. I opened the door and there was a gigantic fly. Suddenly, my ring started to flash. I had never seen it do that before. I started to turn into a gigantic spider. I killed the fly and it turned into a small, silver fly pendant. I found my way out of the house. I took the silver fly pendant and gave it to Hannah. She got it off me and just threw it. Then Hannah said, 'Thanks to you I'm free, but now you'll be trapped in that house forever, unless a girl kisses your marbled, carved face. I've been trapped here for two years and nobody has come except you, now *you* will be a ghost until somebody kisses you.'

Saharish Hafeez (14)
Walthamstow School For Girls, Walthamstow

THE RING OF AMORIANA

'We dare you,' said Lucy.
'But I don't want to go into that house, it's creepy.'
'You have to it's a dare.'
I looked at the big house, I couldn't believe I was actually going in their after all the stories that I had heard . . . I walked slowly to the door, I opened it and peered in. It was completely empty except for spiders which had chosen corners of the room for their home. I walked into a large room. I heard the door shut behind me. I turned around. I desperately tried to open the door, but it wouldn't budge. I made a mental note to myself to kill Lucy once I found a way out. I walked to the back room where I found a door. What would be on the other side?

I opened the door and all I found was a small room. I looked around, but what I saw made me freeze; it made the hairs on the back of my neck stand up. It was a girl, but not any normal girl, she was a ghost. I discovered that I had the use of my legs again. I walked backwards, I heard a floorboard creak.
'I'm sorry, I didn't mean to scare you,' she said.
'My friends have played a joke on me,' I replied. I looked into the girl's eyes and I saw them fill with tears.
'It's nothing you have done. You remind me of myself when I was alive.'
I stood quiet for a moment, thinking of what to say. 'Why are you here?' I said.

She began to tell me her story, 'When I was about 14, I fell ill with tuberculosis. There was no cure and my time left was not long. My mother, being a witch, decided to find a solution to our problem. My mum discovered the Ring Of Amoriana. It gives eternal life to the beholder. My mum gave it to me, but my terrible uncle took it and wore it, leaving me dead. He killed my mother, but her body was never found, so I am stuck here, but my mother preparing for this, hid a cross amulet which does the same thing. If I find it, then I will live again.' As she finished, her voice went croaky and she started to weep.

I decided to help her. 'I will help you to find the amulet,' I replied.

So I began my search for the amulet. Finally I looked in a jewellery box, the amulet was inside. I ran into the room where the girl was. I held the amulet in the air. Her face immediately lit up with a smile, she grabbed my hand and held it tight. The amulet began to glow, I felt myself getting dizzy. What was happening? I fell to the floor. The girl was human, solid, no longer a ghost. I looked at my hand. I could see through it. I was a ghost.
'I'm sorry,' she said, 'but I needed human energy to live.' She walked out of the house and I was left there to haunt the house forever and ever . . .

Charlotte Reynolds (12)
Walthamstow School For Girls, Walthamstow

SARA'S FAVOURITE DAY BECAME HER WORST DAY

It was the last day of the summer term at Sara's school. All the Year 9s were excited, everyone was excited because of course, they were looking forward to their six weeks holiday. There were a few minutes left for the bell to go, everyone was sitting very calmly with their coats on, just waiting for that bell to ring so they could get out of that crusty door. Then the bell rang, everyone jumped out of their seats, pushing and shoving through the crowds.

Sara started walking home with Stacy and Anna, her friends. They always walked home together, but Sara lived the furthest away; they were just telling each other what they were going to do during the holidays. Then Stacy's home came, so she turned into her road. Sara and Anna stopped at the shops to buy some sweets. They were munching away and chatting at the same time. Then finally, Anna's road also came, so she turned.

Now it was Sara left all alone, but she was alright, because she walked home every day. It was not a new thing. Sara really did not like walking the main road way because she thought it was long. Sara preferred the side roads to anything else. There was also a house on one of the side roads, which everyone called 'The Haunted House'. The house had windows covered with pieces of wood and the paint was all crumbling off. It was in a terrible state from outside. An old lady used to live there long before, about nine years ago. The old lady died, and no one lived in that house anymore.

Sara was walking away, minding her own business. As she walked past the house, she heard somebody call out in a spooky voice, 'Come here, little girl.'
Sara looked back, but she did not hear anything. She carried on walking and heard someone call out again, 'Little girl, why don't you listen to me? Come here, I need your help.' Sara was terrified, shocked and sweating with fear.
Then she started walking fast and tried to ignore the fact of her being called. Sara finally reached the main road. She felt relieved after all that. That was one of Sara's worst days; she had never experienced such a scary thing in her life.

When Sara reached home, she was glad that her mum was back from work. Then she was a bit confused whether to tell her mum what had happened. If she told, her mum would have said, 'I told you to always stick to the main roads.' Sara felt she had to share her fear with her mum, she felt much better. Her mum did not know whether it was true, or if Sara was just imagining it. Sara thought to herself, *this will make my whole six-week holiday a misery.*

Attiya Ahmed (14)
Walthamstow School For Girls, Walthamstow

TECHNOPUNZEL
A Fairy Tale For The 21st Century

Technopunzel sat as usual at her laptop and as usual her mother was pestering her about her appearance.
'Darling, why don't you just get a haircut? Or a manicure? Maybe get some nice clothes. At least get off that stupid laptop!' she nagged, applying rather a lot of lipstick to her already pink lips.
'Mum, I don't want a make-over, I've almost finished my anti-gravity machine!' snapped Technopunzel.
Lila (her mum) gave her a sly look, adjusted her cashmere sweater and said, 'You'll never get a husband, looking like that, and those glasses dear, are they really necessary?'
Technopunzel blushed. Her mother had always been able to do that. Technopunzel had incredibly long, greasy, brown hair, large green eyes (her best feature) which were covered by big, jam-jar glasses. She had a short, stubby nose and a few spots. Not much to look at, or so she thought.

That night, Tecnopunzel went to bed happily and was awoken from a deep sleep in the early hours of the morning by a piercing scream. Technopunzel threw off her Winnie the Pooh duvet cover and raced down the stairs to find her mother bent over, bawling her eyes out.
'What's wrong?' she gasped, over the wails.
'My lipstick!' screamed her mother dramatically. 'It's gone, stolen! By that evil scientist next door!'
Anybody would think that Lila was being ridiculous, but Technopunzel knew how much her mother treasured that lipstick (it as very rare). So she ran right out of the house and into her neighbour's back garden (still in her nightie).

Dr Expideath was known as the cleverest, most evil scientist in the country. Technopunzel was very scared of him, but she was going to sneak in the back way to get the lipstick. He was probably using it for one of his awful experiments. She climbed up the fence (with difficulty) and looked through the window. It was a strange room; made completely from metal, and deserted. In the middle of the floor was her mother's precious lipstick. She opened the window (which was strangely easy, considering how clever Dr Expideath was) and climbed in, but the moment her feet touched the smooth, cold metal, and ear-splitting alarm rang through the house and the window sealed shut with an electric lock. There was no door.

Technopunzel froze and a sickening panic rose in her stomach. A hatch in the floor opened and up came Dr Expideath. He looked menacing, with a twisted, evil grin on his face. 'At last I have the final part to my experiment!' he hissed, and suddenly, Technopunzel was jolted into a huge elevator - like a machine that had a tiny space just big enough for her to fit inside. The door slammed and she felt herself spinning so fast she could hardly breathe, but in a matter of seconds she found herself in yet another metal room. 'You will stay here forever!' cried Dr Expideath and he pushed a button. A door opened and he left. It slammed shut immediately. Technopunzel ran to the door and pressed the button; it was worth a try.

'DNA rejected,' said a very electronic voice.

Technopunzel burst into tears. She slumped down on her bed, but immediately got back up again. There were iron springs sticking up from it and the mattress was covered in mould. She inched away from it in case it carried some weird gadget and looked out of the window instead. She really wished she hadn't. Technopunzel had a fear of heights and this tower was . . . high. She slept on the floor that night.

Technopunzel was in the tower for a couple of days, when she heard a sound below her window. Reluctantly, she looked out and saw a man about her age. Her heart leapt and she wiped the tears from her eyes.

'Hello, I'm up here!' she cried.

The man looked up. He had glasses over blue eyes, short black hair and was very pale.

'I've come to rescue you,' he said. 'I know you are Technopunzel, I heard from your mother that Dr Expideath had you imprisoned! My name is Matt Matter. I think the door opens on a DNA sample machine.'

'That's right!' Technopunzel shouted. She had to stop herself dancing on the spot!

Matt looked thoughtful. After a while, he cried, 'Let down your hair!'

Technopunzel blinked. What was he going to do, climb up her hair? That was all very well in a fairy tale, but this was real life. It just wasn't logical. All the same, she let down her hair. It almost reached long enough for Matt to grab hold of the end, but not quite. After several attempts, he got some kind of gadget, pressed a button and suddenly his car drew up. It was a Vauxhall Astra. He stood on top of it and reached her hair.

Technopunzel winced. She looked down and saw that he had out a pair of scissors in his hand. He snipped off a bit of her hair and with it, he went to a laptop in his car. After ten minutes, he came out and cried, 'Try the button now!'

So she did. It worked! She ran down a long metal staircase and up to Matt Matter.

'I locked your DNA sample into the computer database, so you could get out!' he gabbled, looking very pleased with himself.

'Thank you! But what about Dr Expideath?' she gasped.

'I doubt we will be seeing him for a while,' said Matt, blushing.

They drove off together in Matt's car (which was very interesting) and soon after, they got married. You could almost say, they lived happily ever after.

Hannah Taylor-Young (12)
Walthamstow School For Girls, Walthamstow

REALITY

It was a cold and rainy Saturday when Mum had a late shift and Dad was out with his friends. Mum had left me a five-pound note to get some sweets and a video. So before Dad left, Dad and I went to the video shop together. I rented out a film called 'Reality!' Dad left me at 8:30, which left me at home alone. I put the film on and got comfortable. Halfway through the film, I heard the door open. I called out, 'Dad?' but no one answered me, so then I called out, 'Mum?' and still no one answered me. So I got up and walked to the kitchen door, the kitchen door that led to the garden. I looked and no one was there. I just shut the door and came back in. I started to watch the film again.

Ten minutes later, I heard something go *bang* from upstairs. I stood at the bottom of the staircase and shouted, 'Who's up there?' but no one answered me. I grabbed my baseball bat from the bottom cellar and slowly I walked up the stairs. I looked at the bedrooms and all the doors were shut, except for mine. Gently, I pushed open the door and looked, there on the floor was my little glass jar that my nan had made me before she passed away. It was smashed. Sadly, I put down my baseball bat and picked up al the tiny smashed bits of glass. I don't know why, but I felt as if someone was watching me. I sharply turned my head to see if anyone was there.

Suddenly, I heard someone call my name from the bottom of the staircase. I ran to the banister and peered over and there in shock, I saw a dark shadow move from the dining room to the living room. I wiped my eyes and tried to pretend that I didn't see anything. I went downstairs and tried to watch the film again. But . . . the doorbell rang. I ran to the door and looked through the spy hole and could not see anyone, so I opened the door and still no one was there.

By now I was really scared and freaked out. I wished that I had asked my dad to stay home with me. By now, I switched off the TV, I wanted to shut out all of the things that were happening, so I went upstairs and shut all the curtains and locked all the doors. I went to bed. Eventually I fell asleep. I don't know why, but I woke up and saw I was in a coffin.

Aneeka Akhlaq (14)
Walthamstow School For Girls, Walthamstow

A Deadly Dare

Hi, my name is Angel and I am popular in my school because I always win dares. I accept dares to prove that I am the bravest, but I am afraid of this graveyard and that creepy mansion in it.

This new girl in my class, Samantha, she dared me to go and stay for the night all alone in that creepy mansion. I was scared and didn't want to accept it. If I didn't, that would mean I would lose from a girl.

My first night in the mansion, the entire place was so spooky. I could see the full moon from the mansion's window. I was dead scared. I made myself comfortable in that horrible place. I just heard a loud noise, it was that big, old-fashioned clock in front of me. It was midnight, I couldn't go to sleep. I heard a noise, someone saying, 'Cruel people, why did you kill me? I only wanted to ask for forgiveness from my mum,' and he kept repeating this over and over again. I got up and I saw a ghost who was badly injured in front of me. He was in pain, he was walking to a room in the mansion. So I got a bit brave and followed him into the room. He showed me this vision of him getting married to a really rich girl, and his mother who was very proud of him, but everything changed after one day his wife was very rude to his mother and they both fought all the time. He would come home from work and hear their complaints, then his wife said that she wouldn't live with him. That was all I saw that day and I was more confident about going to the mansion again. I wanted to go and help the ghost who was stuck in the mansion.

Next day, I went to school. I told only my friends, but they didn't believe me and that's why I decided to go in the mansion again, and this time I took a camera to take pictures. I saw the same thing that night. I went in that room with him and I saw the vision that he had showed me, that he and his wife moved out of the house and he left his mum. When he was away at work, his wife slept with this other man and he saw them together. Then he took his car and started driving to go and say sorry to his mum. He had an accident and he died, that's why he was stuck in here.

I said to him that his mum had forgiven him and that his mum was waiting in Heaven for him. After I said that, he disappeared.

All the pictures I took, none of them came out. When I went to school the next day, everyone was happy to see me and they said that I was brave. Samantha and I started going out with each other after she said sorry to me. Guess I am still the king.

Farah Akhter (15)
Walthamstow School For Girls, Walthamstow

HOME YET?

Alana ran towards the light with outstretched arms. She could see her parents at the end of the long corridor. What was she doing? Her parents were dead. Dead as could be. They had died just after she was born. She had only seen them in photos that her grandmother kept around the house.

Then what was happening now? How could she see them as clear as day, just a bit further down the hallway? She stopped running; she put her arms down and looked at everyone that was waiting for her. They were all dead, every last one of them. There was Grandpa Alfie and Uncle Jim, all her family that had died. Alana turned around. She ran. Then everything was black.

It was as if she was sleeping but really didn't want to or need to. She thought of her grandmother and how much she would be worrying. She thought of her parents at the end of that corridor. What if she never woke up? Maybe this was her punishment for not going to her dead family members.

Alana felt a bizarre, unnatural force pulling her upwards. It was as if she was a baby and her mother was lifting her out of bed to give her a cuddle. It was something she hadn't experienced, but it was not surprising. Nothing seemed to surprise her anymore. She tried to open her eyes, but there was a light just in front of her face making it impossible to see anything. It was a different light from the light in the hallway, more artificial. Then the light was switched off and she heard someone say,
'OK, everyone agreed? She's gone? Time of death 17:59. I'll go tell the grandmother.' Then she heard footsteps getting further and further away.

The force got stronger. Then suddenly she was sitting on an operating table with her own body next to her. She got up. She walked through the corridors and no one saw her. She was dead, just like her parents. She got to the family waiting room and looked inside. Her grandmother was there with a young doctor. Tears were in her eyes. Alana went in. The doctor was talking, but her grandmother, she wasn't listening. She looked right at Alana and her old eyes crinkled into a smile.

'I knew you'd come, Alana, my sweet. Send my love to Alfie. Now go. Go and be with your parents, they've always wanted to see you all grown up.'

The doctor looked at her and smirked.

'Grandma, I love you. I'll say hello to everyone from you. Promise you'll come soon. Promise?' Alana felt the bizarre pulling again. She hugged her grandmother and kissed her for the last time. 'Promise?' she said.

'Promise,' the old woman replied.

Then Alana was back in the corridor and this time she knew which way to run. She ran to her parents and hugged them tight. At last she was home.

Louise Bloor (13)
Walthamstow School For Girls, Walthamstow

THE FINAL CURTAIN

Daisy took a deep breath and walked onto the stage. This was the scene where everything had gone wrong last year . . .

19th December 1932

'Come on everyone, this is the final scene in this masterpiece. Flo, Mary, are you ready for action? The audience are waiting for you!' shrilled Mrs Peterson.
Florence and Mary stepped out from behind the curtains and looked out at the audience. They weren't too nervous, Longfield Boarding School did a production of 'Peter Pan' every Christmas, so the audience knew what to expect.
'Prepare to die Peter Pan!' grinned Mary, who made a brilliant Captain Hook, maybe even too brilliant.
'I have nothing to say to you except I think we both know a certain crocodile!' cried Flo.
'Cr-cr-crocodile?' stuttered Mary.

Suddenly, there was a gunshot. It cracked through the air like a knife. Mary staggered to the ground. Blood spewed everywhere. There were screams from the audience. Mary couldn't believe it, it had happened *again!*

One year later . . .

As Daisy stepped into the bright lights of the stage, her stomach turned. It wasn't because she was nervous about playing the lead in the legendary production, it was because she and her friends had a plan and it was vital it worked. The school's drama department chose 'Peter Pan' every year because one of the leading characters was a ghost.

It had all started twenty years ago when the school first decided to do 'Peter Pan' as the Christmas play and Mary, the girl who played Captain Hook, had been killed. No one knew who had done it and the police had called it a mystery, but every year since then, Mary's ghost returned and the tragedy had repeated itself. What Daisy didn't understand was why the teachers wouldn't do anything about it. They seemed to just hope that it would all sort itself out. But she and her friends, Mabel and Alice, wanted to do something about it. They had a theory that if Mary could finish the play without being shot, she would be able to leave this world peacefully. So Mabel and Alice were guarding the entrance with the help of a gun Alice had stolen off her father (which was left over from the war) and Mabel's dog, Bruiser.

'Cr-cr-crocodile?'
She'd said it: those terrible words. Daisy could feel the whole audience holding their breath with her. There was no gunshot. They'd done it! The rest of the play passed in a blur, and as the final curtain fell, Daisy turned just in time to see Mary disappear like she'd never even existed.

It turned out that Mabel and Alice had only caught a glimpse of the killer. They'd scared him off with the gun and Bruiser baring his teeth. So the murderer's identity was still a mystery. They had saved the school and Mary from an eternity of 'Peter Pan', which everyone would be grateful for!

Kate Turner (13)
Walthamstow School For Girls, Walthamstow

REVENGE

It was midnight in Point Harbour and Angeline was all alone on the beach. The beach was the main attraction in Point Harbour, it was well known for its beautiful scenery and strange past.

Angeline had just recently moved there. She was only 16 and had already committed the biggest sin anyone could ever commit, she had murdered someone and that someone was Lee Michaels. She stood on the beach, the wet sand cooling down her feet from all the running she had done today. She tried to clear her mind and think of everything that had happened. It had all started on the 13th of December when she had just moved to Point Harbour . . .

I didn't want to move. The old Wilkinson house gave me the creeps, but I was especially upset that day because my mum Linda was ill and my dad Tom wasn't home yet. He had gone out to get her medicine and hadn't come home. It was getting late, I didn't tell Mum, she would worry too much. Later that night, I heard the doorbell ring, only to find Dad lying unconscious on the floor.

The next day at the hospital, Dad woke up. He had said that the only thing he could remember was being hit on the back of the head with a large object. Mum was told to stay at home, she wasn't feeling well. Dad decided not to report it to the police and was allowed to go home. When we got home, we found Mum hiding in the basement. She said that she had heard strange noises downstairs and decided to investigate, but as she approached the balcony, she heard someone mumbling and could only make out the word 'revenge', that's when she'd decided to hide.

A few months later, everything was forgotten. I had made quite a lot of friends those few months and one of them was Lee Michaels.

Me and Lee decided to meet up at my house to watch a movie. While we waited for the movie to come on, I went to the kitchen to get some popcorn. As I moved towards the kitchen, I noticed the chopping knife missing, only to find out where it had gone. Suddenly, I heard a scream and Lee came in, the chopping knife in his stomach. I watched in horror as he lay dying in front of me. I ran as fast as I could away from all the commotion.

I stood there on the beach with a guilty conscience and realised why Lee had been acting so strangely. He must have found out everything, I had to go back. I stepped into the house and felt his force overpowering me. Finally I was free of his ghost, my father John Wilkinson could rest at peace. That poor soul who was thrown off the balcony by my stepparents, Linda and Tom.

I had fulfilled my father's wishes, I had taken *revenge.*

Humaa Kazim
Walthamstow School For Girls, Walthamstow

ONCE UPON A DEATH

This is no fairy tale: this is a true story about a girl whose uncle collected the souls of ghosts . . .

Tia was a sixteen-year-old girl who lived a normal life with her mum, her dad passed away when she was a baby. Tia did art in college, it was her last year and she still didn't have a boyfriend. Tia was so beautiful and she was one of the only girls in her college who didn't have a boyfriend, that's why everyone looked at her like she was some sort of geek.

One day, Tia's mum was coming home form work and, out of nowhere, a car came and crashed into her and Tia's mum was lying in hospital, dead. Tia was devastated when she heard. Tia had no choice but to go and live with her uncle, who lived somewhere in the middle of Texas.

The next day, Tia set off for Texas. Now Tia's uncle came from the rich side of the family, that's why a car came to pick her up. The car just dropped her and her bags off, but didn't stop. Tia went into the house and a guy was standing in front of her, and for Tia it was love at first sight. Then Tia's uncle came and showed her around and explained that Kevin (the guy) was living there with him. The house was odd because from the inside it was all made from glass, but it was a massive house though and so beautiful.

So far, Tia was loving it there (at her uncle's) especially when Kevin was there. It was her third day living there and she and Kevin were getting closer each minute. Tia was sitting on the garden bench with Kevin, it was getting cold so Kevin wrapped his arms around her. They started talking and then they started kissing! Tia had finally got a boyfriend and Kevin had done the job he was meant to do for her uncle.

The next morning, Tia woke up and she could hear someone calling her, so she got up and followed the sound. She followed it and she was just walking forward when one of the glass walls moved in front of her and blocked her way. She turned around and something pulled her up against the wall and hit her harder and harder, so hard that her blood was dripping everywhere. Tia was lying there when Kevin came and picked her up. Kevin took her to the main room where all the ghosts stood. There was a circle of them.

What Tia didn't know was that her uncle collected souls for a living and sold them to the Devil. He only collected pure souls and turned them evil. Now, Tia's uncle needed thirteen ghosts and he had twelve, the last ghost was Tia who had a pure heart. The thirteenth ghost had to join the circle by love only and that was why Kevin had fallen in love with her.

It was time. The circle was spinning. Kevin stepped into place. It was Tia's turn to step forward. Kevin put his hand out and her love for him killed her . . .

Maryam Hussain (13)
Walthamstow School For Girls, Walthamstow

HENDERSON HOUSE

Henderson House is haunted.

The house stands on the edge of my street, it's huge. Victorian-style, the windows are boarded and the garden overgrown. It's called Henderson House because the Henderson family died there 20 years ago. It was a fire, nobody ever found out how it started. Terrible tragedy it may seem, but the truth is, nobody liked the Hendersons. They were thought to be nosy and snobbish, that's why not everybody thinks the fire was an accident. I can see Henderson House from my bedroom window, and sometimes if I'm really still, I can see flames at the windows.

But that's not as bad as what I saw last summer. I was taking my dog Jack for a walk, we had just got past the house when he froze. 'Come on Jack,' I urged, thinking he had seen another cat, but he started barking and then he ran. I tore after him. He ran past the shops, past the hairdresser's and straight into the back garden of the house. I soon spotted Jack cowering under the old shed. I ran through the jungle of grass towards him and soon discovered that he was shaking and was whining.

When I reached him, I saw what Jack was scared of. I bent down to take a closer look and it took me a while to work out what it was, and then it hit me. It has a hand, the bones of a skeleton hand.

I screamed and I picked up Jack and ran. We ran back through the jungle of grass. I then started to panic. It was dark and I didn't even know if I was going in the right direction. I looked back and saw Mr Henderson's ghost sitting on the shed, he only had one hand. I shuddered and began to cry. I finally came to my house and burst through the door. I was crying, screaming, shouting.

I don't take Jack for a walk anymore; I draw my curtains as soon as it gets dark and try never to look at the house. So it's like I said before: the Henderson house is haunted.

Jennifer Hassan (13)
Walthamstow School For Girls, Walthamstow

VAMPIRE...

The night was cold and dark. A chilly wind was blowing through a gap in the shutters at my window. I could hear nothing but the distant sound of the cars on the motorway. I could taste the dust in the air. The darkness played tricks on my eyes, making strange, ghostly shapes in my glass cabinet.

I lay in my bed, wide awake, wrapped mummy-like in my blankets. Something was making a scratching, scraping noise on one of my bed posts. I started to breathe heavily and my heart started to beat faster. I daren't look round or sit up. I was too scared to move, practically nailed to the bed by fear. I could have sworn that something had moved in the corner of my eye.

All of a sudden, a black figure jumped onto my bed and leant over me. I would have screamed, but I was so petrified that my voice was stuck in my throat. All I could hear was its long, rattling breath, which stank of something dead. Its eyes glowed red and its mouth was forming a sly smile. A sly smile with fangs. It was a vampire! It drew closer, my heart beat more ferociously. The vampire raised its hand and placed it on my arm, which was hanging out of the blankets. I had broken it whilst on my bike the other day. My arm started to tingle. The cast loosened and slipped off. I could feel the bones healing under my skin. I moved it. It was fixed! Completely back to normal! 'Thanks,' I said to the vampire.
'Now do something for me,' he hissed.
'Like what?'
'Fetch me blood!'
I gasped. 'What blood?' I asked.
'Human blood!' said the vampire, and he clicked his fingers.

Suddenly, I was outside in the freezing cold, in my coat and pyjamas. I had a strange power inside that took over me, as though I was the bee and blood was my nectar . . .

A woman in a blue coat walked past. I ran over to her. I felt two long sharp things growing from my mouth. There was a scream and then I was back in my room. I handed the vampire a glass full of red liquid. He drank it in three gulps.
'Thank you!' he hissed.

But I knew that it wasn't enough for him. I knew that he would make me get more that same night. Then my housemate walked through the door and the vampire *did* make me get more. But this time I had to get some blood from her . . . and I made sure he got it . . .

Kayleigh Chambers (11)
Wesley Green School, Oxford